Applying Numbers and IT in

Leisure and Tourism

Also available from Cassell:

Cox: *An Introduction to Office Management for Secretaries*

Doolan: *Applying Numbers and IT in Health and Social Care*

Goddard: *Informative Writing, 2nd edn*

Sharman, Cross and Vennis: *Observing Children: A Practical Guide*

Treby: *An Introduction to Information Technology*

Applying Numbers and IT

IN

Leisure and Tourism

Chris Doolan

CASSELL
London and New York

Cassell

Wellington House, 125 Strand, London WC2R 0BB

370 Lexington Avenue, New York, NY 10017–6550

www.cassell.co.uk

First published 1999

British Library Cataloguing-in-Publication Data

A catalogue record for this book is available from the British Library.

ISBN 0–304–33459–6

Designed and typeset by Ben Cracknell Studios

Printed and bound in Great Britain by Bookcraft (Bath) Ltd, Midsomer Norton

Contents

Introduction

This book is intended to guide you through the Core Skills for Application of Numbers and Information Technology, and the Performance Criteria for the GNVQ in Leisure and Tourism.

If you plan your assignments correctly for mandatory and optional units, you should achieve most if not all of these Core Skills, without the need to produce additional work.

You should think about Core Skills at the planning stage of assignments. If you are in doubt check with your tutor. Careful planning will save you having to do additional work in order to pass the various Core Skills.

Remember that for the GNVQ *you* are required to provide evidence that you have achieved each of the Performance Criteria. Think of ways in which you can provide this evidence and *don't* leave it until the day before the moderator is due to try and convince your tutor that you have done enough!

Some of this evidence will be obvious and your tutor will have no trouble in identifying the Performance Criteria you have achieved. Some Performance Criteria, however, will require a little more effort on your part. If you put yourself in the position of the lecturer, he/she must, in order to pass you for each unit, be able to satisfy himself or herself that sufficient evidence has been provided.

I will begin by introducing you to how the computer works.

How the computer works

When we think of the computer, it is usually as a single unit and includes everything: the keyboard, the visual display unit and the rectangular box into which we insert disks. In fact the box, which is the Central Processing Unit, is the 'brains' of the computer and all the other parts, although they may be necessary, are either input or output devices that are peripheral to the main unit.

As the name suggests, the Central Processing Unit (CPU) is responsible for controlling the processing of data and instructions within the computer system.

The CPU consists of three main sections:

- The *ALU* (Arithmetic and Logic Unit), where all calculations are carried out and logic statements are tested.
- *Main Memory*, which holds instructions and data when the computer is active, i.e. switched on. This memory is *volatile*, which means that if power to the computer is lost for any reason, the memory's contents will be lost. This type of memory is known as *RAM* (Random Access Memory). The capacity of RAM will vary depending on the computer's specification, but the greater the memory, the more efficiently the computer can operate. The fact that RAM is volatile means that it is absolutely vital that as you work you regularly save your files to a permanent storage device. The most common way of doing this is by inserting a *floppy disk* into one of the disk drives in the Central Processing Unit and copying all your work onto it.
- The *Control Unit* manages all instructions, inputs and outputs, and switches data and instructions from storage, such as the computer's hard disk, CD ROM, etc. to main memory, as and when required.

If the control unit did not do its job properly, RAM would soon become full and the unit could not operate.

All computers have *ROM* (Read Only Memory), which is fitted by the manufacturer. This type of memory is designed so that it cannot be overwritten. ROM stores instructions and data which the computer needs all the time, from the moment the computer is switched on.

When you first switch on the computer, it goes through a sequence of self testing to check that input and output devices are connected. Only when this has been done will it load the *Operating System*. The operating system is essential software, and it is through this system software that application software is loaded.

Once the operating system has been loaded, you should be able to select from the various options available on your computer. Systems range from being very modest with limited application software, e.g. a word processor, to the most sophisticated system, linked to a file server with a vast array of application software at your disposal. Your computer may allow you access to the Internet, if you are registered with a carrier such as Compuserve and have a modem, which allows digital (computerized) information to be converted into analogue (sound waves) commonly used on the telephone network.

If you are going to use an input device such as a keyboard, you will be typing in a language which you can understand (*human readable form*) but the computer cannot deal with data in this form and must convert the data into a language that it can understand. Computers use *binary* (zeros and ones), and every key stroke has its own special translation.

Figure 1 shows how information and data flow from input, via the Central Processing Unit, to output devices.

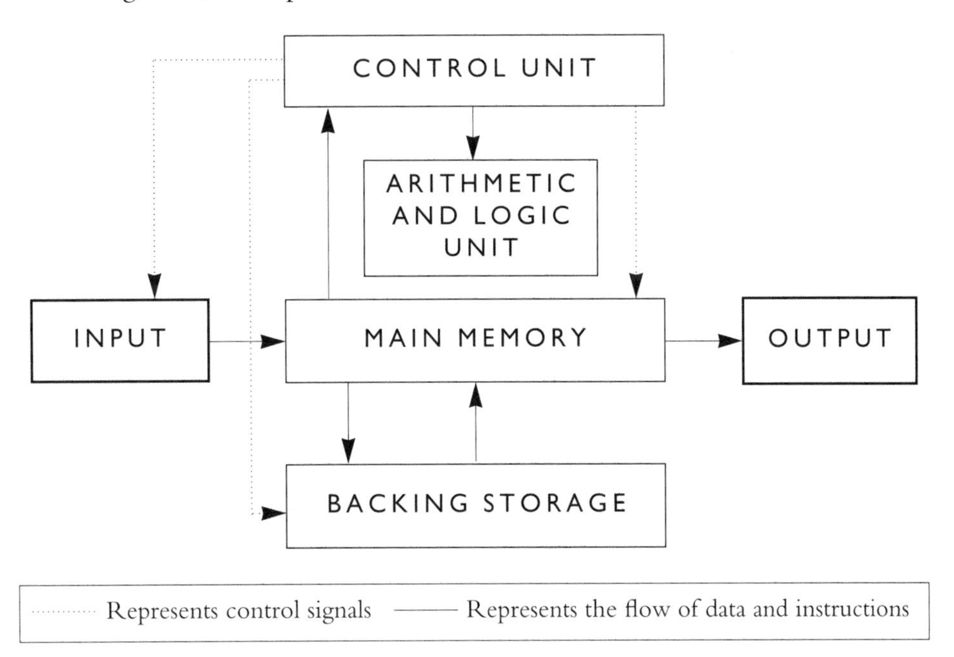

Figure 1 How information and data flow from input to output devices

What happens when you save your work to disk?

Whether you save your work on the computer's hard internal disk or to a floppy disk which you have inserted into one of the CPU's disk drives, the computer must make a note of where it has placed the file.

When you save a file, you are required to give the file a name (in some packages you are limited to a short file name with no spaces allowed); once this has been done, the computer produces a file allocation table and finds a suitable location on the disk.

The floppy disk is made of a circle of black plastic material which has a special magnetic coating. This disk is enclosed within a hard casing which has the read/write head and the drive spindle only visible. The majority of floppy disks measure 3.5 inches but the amount of data which can be stored on them will depend on whether they are high density or not. The word *density* refers to how tightly packed the data are. (It is possible to *compress* data so that a disk will hold well in excess of 1.4 MB.)

Both sides of the floppy disk are organized in concentric tracks running around the disk rather like a vinyl record. The disk is 'divided' into sectors. When you save work, therefore, the computer must decide which side of the disk to use, which sector and which tracks to make use of. Where possible, it will keep all the contents of the file together, but if this is not possible it will split the contents of the file, possibly in another sector.

The computer keeps track of where it saves work by using *addresses*. It will record the first location (address) and add a few characters which will show where the remainder of the file is located. The user should not be aware of any delay when retrieving work which has been stored. However, if the disk becomes too full it is a good idea to begin a new one, as this will allow the computer to work more efficiently.

Some disks come ready formatted. This simply means that they have been set up ready to receive data. If the disk is not formatted then you will have to ask the computer to format the disk, otherwise it will be incapable of storing anything. You only format a disk once – each time you format, it deletes the entire contents of your disk!

1

Application of Number Core Skills

Elements and Performance Criteria relating to the application of numbers

1 Collect and record data

The Application of Number Core Skills, if used correctly, should, in the main, be achieved when planning and producing the main mandatory and optional units of your chosen subject. Only a small amount of additional work may need to be submitted if the Performance Criteria are not naturally achieved.

Use the methods which will be outlined in this chapter to save yourself unnecessary additional work.

You are required to design data collection sheets which display the latest of at least two data collection and measuring tasks:

- at least two tasks involving money
- at least two tasks involving measurement of physical dimensions
- at least two tasks involving data collection/measurement of one other property
- at least two further tasks, each involving measurement of a different rate of change (e.g. speed, inflation rates, etc.).

1.1 *Make decisions about what data should be collected*

The type of data and the method of collecting and collating the data will obviously depend on the task in hand. All decisions will be made at the planning stage and you should include methods to be employed within your planning document which will accompany each assignment.

An excellent way of providing evidence for the Performance Criteria for Application of Number would be to undertake a research project. When you analyse the data you can draw attention to how you

- use your estimating skills by 'intelligent guessing' of what the results of your survey/research project are likely to be (from the data collected);
- express selected data as a fraction of the whole (using fractions and decimal fractions);
- express selected ranges of data as proportions and percentages of the whole;
- compare your estimates against the *actual results* of your research and decide whether your estimating skills were good or poor.

1.2 *Choose and use techniques which suit the task*

You will use the most appropriate method of collecting data from a sample group. You should describe your reasons for choosing your sample group and the measuring instruments used (e.g. weighing, measuring, etc.). You should also use the most appropriate units to describe your results (e.g. height in metres/ centimetres, weight in kilograms/grams, pulse rates in beats per minute, etc.).

1.3 *Perform the techniques in a correct order*

The key to gaining this Performance Criterion is careful, logical planning.

- Decide on the project you wish to research and ensure that a standard method of collecting the data is used.
- If using questionnaires, you should avoid any form of ambiguity (this is not as easy as it sounds).
- Roughly estimate what you *think* the results are likely to be.
- Use tally sheets to note the data extracted from your research.
- Use suitable headings under which your results will be entered.
- Employ the most appropriate form(s) of calculations.

- Check for accuracy.
- Compare actual results against those expected (from your estimates).
- Analyse your results by drawing attention to any extremes of data (e.g. particularly high or low), indicating the range in which the majority of the data lies, etc.

1.4 *Choose and work to an appropriate level of accuracy*

- Any questions used to collect data must be clear and decisive.
- All measuring tools must be accurate.
- Indistinct or spoiled questionnaires should be discarded.
- Care should be taken when collating and recording the data.
- *Never* change the data to suit your argument.

1.5 *Record data in appropriate units and in an appropriate format*

- Use a tally sheet to record results.
- Enter data in a suitable format under clear headings showing their units.

1.6 *Make sure that records are accurate and complete*

- Double check the data recorded from the original source, e.g. questionnaires, etc., and from the tally sheets.
- Ensure that no data have been excluded unless the result is unclear.

1.7 *Identify sources of error and their effects*

- Did any external variables affect your results? (e.g. if recording pulse rates your sample should all have been engaged in the same type of activity immediately before their pulse was taken). A possible cause for error might be if you were collecting data by observing somebody carrying out a task and they were interrupted. This could give misleading results.

2 Tackle problems

2.1 *Choose and use techniques which suit the problem*

The techniques you use to draw conclusions from your data will depend on the type of numbers. These will include the following: working with numbers of any size, using addition, subtraction, multiplication and division; calculating with fractions and decimal fractions and with percentages and ratios; calculating using formulae expressed in words and in symbols and using powers and roots.

2.2 *Perform the techniques in a correct order*

Once you have decided which techniques are most suited to your application, you must perform them in the correct order. For example, if you want to find the mean average within a group of numbers, you must first list the frequency of each data item, then total the data range and divide by the frequency.

2.3 *Choose and use appropriate units*

All calculations should be in the most appropriate units of measurement:

- The perimeter of a shape, for example, is measured in linear units but the two-dimensional area of a plane is measured in square units.
- When solving problems in three dimensions, e.g. when expressing the volume of simple shapes or the volume of cylinders, the result will be in units cubed.
- Calculations with compound measures – e.g. when calculating the strength of materials – could use two different units, e.g. kg per mm^2.

2.4 *Choose and use an appropriate level of accuracy*

The level of accuracy will very much depend on the type of data. For example, the level of accuracy required in manufacturing may be extremely high, while if calculations concern currency it is unlikely that you would go beyond two decimal places.

2.5 *Use mathematical terms correctly*

No matter how well you have carried out your calculations, if you express the mathematical terms incorrectly, your results will be wrong. For example, if you are calculating the area of a sports hall using metres, you must express the result with the symbol m^2 or write 'square metres'.

2.6 *Carry out calculations correctly*

Calculations must be carried out in accordance with standard procedures. For example, if adding or subtracting fractions, you should first find a common denominator and cancel the answer(s) down as appropriate. For example:

$\frac{1}{2} + \frac{1}{4} + \frac{3}{4} = \frac{2}{4} + \frac{1}{4} + \frac{3}{4} = \frac{6}{4} = 1\frac{2}{4} = 1\frac{1}{2}$

When handling data, e.g. ratios and percentages, convert into common units of measurement using scales, tables and calculations, e.g. from imperial to metric. Calculate using mean, median and mode to show that you understand how to find these three different types of averages. Drawing graphs to represent your findings will greatly assist you in describing in which quartile the data are distributed and indicate the skew of the distribution. We will discuss this in greater depth in examples of averages.

2.7 *Carry out checking procedures to confirm the results of calculations*

Always double check the results of your calculations by using a calculator or computer application software. You should then check your own estimates *prior* to calculations with the actual results of your calculations. You could also use inverse operations by using your result and then going back through each stage of the calculations.

2.8 *Check that the results make sense in respect of the problem being tackled*

You *may* be convinced that your calculations are correct but it always pays to check. For example, if you are expressing each frequency of data in terms of percentages, you should total all the percentages together – if the total is greater or less than 100, unless the difference is fractional, you know you have gone wrong somewhere!

2.9 *Identify the effects of any accumulating errors in calculations*

A small error in a single data item may at first glance not appear to be too serious but it can have very serious repercussions. For example, if you are calculating the break-even point, i.e. the point at which no money is made but no money is lost, and an error occurs, the following could happen.

Total fixed overheads £3000	
Manufacturing cost per unit	= £4.00 ★ error
Selling price per unit	= £6.50

★ *Manufacturing cost per unit should read £5.00*

Our fixed overheads remain the same whether we manufacture one or one million units. The variable overheads will be the quantity manufactured multiplied by the manufacturing cost per unit. The revenue (incoming money) will be the quantity purchased multiplied by the selling price per unit. Profit = total revenue less total fixed and variable overheads. Our error that started out at £1 for one unit will be hugely increased and give a very misleading result!

3 Interpret and present data

3.1 *Identify and explain the main features of the data*

The way in which the data are handled will decide whether your work has been successful or not. No matter how careful you have been to collect and collate information accurately, if the handling does not conform to correct practices the results will be misleading.

Once you are satisfied that all calculations have been carried out successfully and that your work is as extensive as possible, covering all of the GNVQ requirements noted in the assignment given by your tutor, you should draw the reader's attention to the main features of your data, for example extremes of data (upper and lower bounds) and the most common. You should express the main relationships and any patterns that have appeared. These expressions should be in written and symbolic form. The relationship between sets of data should be described involving rate, and expressing relationships as equations and inequalities.

Examples of how this can be done will be given in the final section of this book.

3.2 *Choose and use techniques which will present the data effectively*

It is vital that the results of your data analysis are properly presented, in a suitable format. A good way of giving results is by writing a clear, concise report containing tables which detail the results of data. Graphs and/or charts are an excellent addition to the data themselves.

3.3 *Follow conventions for presenting the data*

It is essential that the correct data are used to obtain graphs and that these have suitable headings and axis labels. The type of graph or chart chosen should be suitable for the purpose and we will discuss this in the last section of this book.

3.4 *Present the results with an appropriate level of accuracy*

Care should be taken when presenting data that accuracy is as good as is feasibly possible by selecting and using appropriate units for presenting data and selecting and using appropriate scales.

3.5 *Explain how the results make sense in respect of the problem being tackled*

Whenever giving results, you must be able to justify them. This means that the reader should be reminded of the methods decided on at the planning stage for collecting and recording data. You should be able to justify the calculations carried out on the data and be able to prove that the final results are valid.

2

Theory and Practice in Application of Numbers

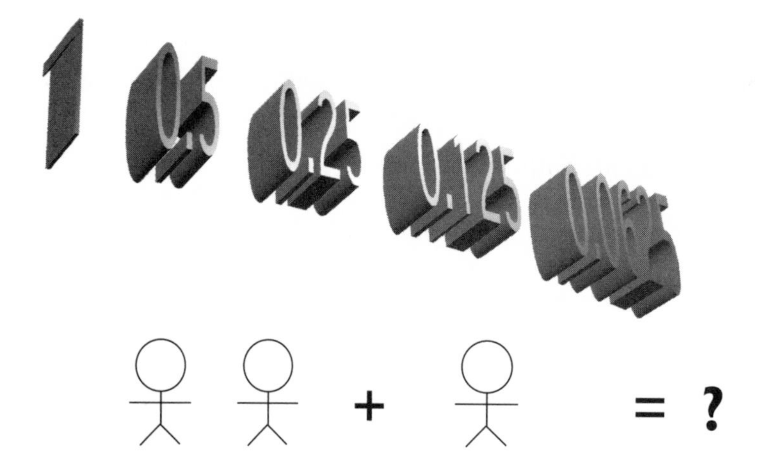

Whether you have always hated maths or simply need your memory jogging, this section of the book will help you. Some things you will find very easy, some more difficult. The key to success is practice, and several questions will be given at the end of each section to test those brain cells.

What's in a number?

There are many different types of number, ranging from whole numbers, called integers, to fractions and decimals.

There are other numbers which cover a logical range and special names are assigned to these types.

Prime numbers: numbers which can only be divided either by 1 or themselves.

Examples: 1, 2, 3, 5, 7, 11, 13, 17, 19, 23, 29 – find the next number in the range.

Square numbers: the result of numbers which have been squared, i.e. multiplied by themselves.

Examples: 1 (1 × 1), 4 (2 × 2), 9 (3 × 3), 16 (4 × 4), 25 (5 × 5), 36 (6 × 6) – find the next three square numbers in the range.

Triangular numbers: numbers which can form a triangle.

Examples:

1	•
3	• •
6	• • •
10	• • • •
15	• • • • •
21	• • • • • •

See if you can find the next two triangular numbers.

Addition, subtraction, multiplication and division

Here are four types of arithmetic that we do on a regular daily basis and we all remember how to do them:

$2 + 2 = 4$ $4 - 2 = 2$ $6 \times 2 = 12$ $12 \div 2 = 6$

Easy, isn't it! Life gets a little trickier when we deal with larger numbers or have to subtract a larger number from a smaller one.

$1234 + 300 + 6999 + 1256 + 7 + 9999$

The first thing to do is to make sure that you line up your column of figures correctly. If you get it wrong, you will get the wrong result. Remember, you must always work from right to left and any carried units must not be ignored.

```
 1234
  300
 6999
 1256
    7
 9999
-----
19795
```

How do you subtract 61 from 45? The calculator can do it in a second, but could you manage it without the calculator? There is an easy tip: take the smaller number away from the larger number, but remember to change the sign, i.e. the number becomes negative, just like your bank balance when you become overdrawn (see Figure 2.1).

	Date	Debit	Credit	Balance
Brought forward				£1300.00
Pay cheque	30.09.97		£985.00	£2285.00
Mortgage	02.10.97	£520.47		£1764.53
Holiday	07.10.97	£1800.00		–£35.47
Bonus	09.10.97		£350.00	£314.53

Credit = money you receive
Debit = money you pay
Balance = the result after dealing with credits and debits

Figure 2.1 Checking your bank balance

You will notice that by adding a positive figure (the bonus of £350) to the negative figure of –£35.47 we get a positive balance of £314.53.

Multiplication

Learn your times tables! It may be boring but it makes calculations so much easier, especially for day-to-day arithmetic such as shopping.

When multiplying very large numbers together it is easy to get lost. There are many different methods of multiplication. Look at the two examples below and see which you find easiest.

```
    14567
   × 3999
   131103
  131103
 131103
 43701
 --------
 58253433
```

The method we used here was to multiply 14567 by the first 9 (the least significant digit). We then moved one place to the left and multiplied 14567 by the second 9. We moved one further place to the left and multiplied 14567 by the third 9. Finally we moved one further place to the left and multiplied 14567 by 3 (the most significant digit).

Once this had been done we simply totalled the figures together in order to get the whole answer.

```
    14567
   × 3999
   131103
  1311030
 13110300
 43701000
 --------
 58253433
```

With this example you will notice that instead of moving one place to the left each time we inserted zeros, one to replace each move.

Division

You will need to know your tables here too!

We will begin with a nice friendly division with no remainders to cause problems:

864 ÷ 8

We start this time from the left. How many times does 8 go into 8? Once exactly with no remainder – so we put down our 1 and move to the next number to the right. How many times does 8 go into 6? It doesn't – it isn't large enough.

We cannot ignore it, so we put a 0 and we bring the last number to the right together with the 6 to form the number 64 and ask: how many times does 8 go into 64? 8 times exactly, and so we assemble the results and find that 8 goes into 864 exactly 108 times. Check it out on the calculator.

Few people like long division, but if you line everything up properly you will find that it is not too bad.

95464 ÷ 78

Just as with the normal, short division sum, we need to find how many times 78 will divide into 95464. This time we won't be as lucky, we will have tricky remainders to deal with. This is the method we use. We begin from the left hand side (the most significant digit). The sum is broken down into manageable parts. We see how many 78s there are in each part; this figure is noted and the balance subtracted; we then move down the next digit.

Step 1

Moving from the left, the first number greater than 78 is 95.

78 into 95 goes only once and so we put 1 to form part of the answer and deduct 78 from 95, leaving a remainder of 17.

We then bring down the next digit (4), making 174.

```
      1
78) 95464
   -78
    174
```

Step 2

78 into 174 goes twice ($2 \times 78 = 156$) so we put 2 to form part of the answer and deduct 156 from 174, leaving a remainder of 18.

We then bring down the next digit (6), making 186.

```
      12
78) 95464
   -78
    174
   -156
     186
```

Step 3

78 into 186 goes twice ($2 \times 78 = 156$) so we put 2 to form part of the answer and deduct 156 from 186, leaving a remainder of 30.

We then bring down the next digit (4), making 304.

```
      122
78) 95464
   -78
    174
   -156
     186
    -156
      304
```

Step 4

78 into 304 goes three times ($3 \times 78 = 234$), so we put 3 to form part of our answer and deduct 234 from 304 leaving a remainder of 70.

We have now used up each of the digits but still have a remainder of 70. This must not be ignored and so we need to continue with our calculation. We place a decimal point after the last digit of our answer. We now need to add a 0 to our remainder to give a number that can be divided by 78.

```
      1223
78) 95464
    -78
     174
    -156
      186
     -156
       304
      -234
        700
```

The number of decimal places we work to will depend on the level of accuracy required.

By adding a 0 after our remainder of 70, this gives a figure of 700.

Step 5

78 into 700 goes 8 times, so we place an 8 after the decimal point ($8 \times 78 = 624$). We subtract 624 from 700 which leaves a remainder of 76.

We add a 0 to this figure in order that we can continue: 760.

```
      1223.8
78) 95464
    -78
     174
    -156
      186
     -156
       304
      -234
        700
       -624
         760
```

Step 6

78 into 760 goes 9 times. We place a nine at the end of our answer ($9 \times 78 = 702$).

We subtract 702 from 760 which leaves a remainder of 58.

We add a 0 to this figure to give 580.

```
      1223.89
78) 95464
    -78
     174
    -156
      186
     -156
       304
      -234
        700
       -624
         760
        -702
          580
```

Step 7

78 into 580 goes 7 times. We add the number 7 to our answer (7 × 78 = 546). If we subtract 546 from 580 we have a remainder of 34. If we wanted to continue we would add a 0 to make it 340 and continue to divide by 78. The level of accuracy required will determine how many decimal places you will take the calculation to.

```
          1223.897
78)  95464
    -78
     174
    -156
      186
     -156
       304
      -234
        700
       -624
         760
        -702
          580
         -546
remainder  34
```

Try a few more:

1. 1259 ÷ 156
2. 555 ÷ 20
3. 5009 ÷ 50

Check your results:

1. 8.0705128 (depending on the level of accuracy required, you could limit the number of decimal places)
2. 27.75
3. 100.18

Getting started on fractions

Everybody can easily calculate simple fractions such as $\frac{1}{2}$, $\frac{1}{4}$, or even $\frac{1}{8}$ but may worry when the fractions are slightly more complex. The same rules always apply. To find a half of something you need to divide by 2; to find a quarter you divide by 4 and to find an eighth you divide by 8. Once you have done this, it is then very simple to find other fractions within the range. To find $\frac{3}{8}$ you first divide by 8 to find $\frac{1}{8}$ and then multiply the result by 3, giving you $\frac{3}{8}$.

Try the following simple questions and check your answers against those below:

1. What is $\frac{1}{4}$ of 16?
2. What are $\frac{3}{4}$ of 16?
3. What is $\frac{1}{16}$ of 48?
4. What are $\frac{15}{16}$ of 48?
5. What are $\frac{5}{8}$ of 80?
6. What are $\frac{3}{8}$ of 100?

Answers

1. 4
2. 12
3. 3
4. 45
5. 50
6. 37.5

Adding, subtracting, multiplying and dividing fractions

If you were to be asked to add $\frac{1}{2}$ and $\frac{1}{4}$ together, you would be able to say that the answer was $\frac{3}{4}$ – you will have done the sum without even thinking of the method used.

In order to add or subtract fractions you must first bring the fractions to a value by which both fractions can be expressed, otherwise it is rather like saying add 1 cherry and 1 apple. The only answer to this sum is 2 pieces of fruit – not very useful!

You first need to find a *common denominator*, i.e. base figure. Since $\frac{1}{2}$ is greater than $\frac{1}{4}$, it is obvious that you will need to convert the halves into quarters before you can begin: $\frac{1}{2} = \frac{2}{4}$. You then add $\frac{2}{4}$ to $\frac{1}{4}$ and get a result of $\frac{3}{4}$.

What about this problem? Add $\frac{1}{4}$, $\frac{3}{8}$ and $\frac{1}{16}$ together. The lowest common denominator in this case is 16.

There are 4×4 in 16, and 2×8 in 16. Whatever you have done to the denominator you must do to the top figure, so:

$1 \times 4 = 4$
$3 \times 2 = 6$
$1 \times 1 = 1$

You now simply add these results together, remembering to use the common denominator, and you have the answer, $\frac{11}{16}$. This number does not need to be cancelled down since the fraction is not top heavy (the top number is not larger than the lower number) and 11 won't divide evenly into 16.

Exactly the same method is used to subtract fractions. Try the following:

1. $\frac{1}{2} + \frac{1}{4} + \frac{5}{8}$
2. $\frac{1}{3} + \frac{1}{8}$
3. $\frac{2}{3} + \frac{1}{4} + \frac{5}{8}$
4. $\frac{15}{16} - \frac{1}{4}$
5. $\frac{7}{8} - \frac{2}{3}$
6. $\frac{6}{7} - \frac{1}{3}$

Answers

1. $\frac{11}{8}$. Cancel down (11 divided by 8) = 1 remainder 3 = $1\frac{3}{8}$
2. 3 will not divide equally into 8 and so the lowest common denominator becomes 24; adjust the top figures to match. $\frac{8}{24} + \frac{3}{24} = \frac{11}{24}$
3. The lowest common denominator is 24, i.e. 24 will divide by each of the denominators. 24 ÷ 3 = 8; 24 ÷ 4 = 6; 24 ÷ 8 = 3; The next stage is to adjust each fraction into 24ths: $\frac{2}{3} = \frac{16}{24}$; $\frac{1}{4} = \frac{6}{24}$; $\frac{5}{8} = \frac{15}{24}$. We can now add them together: 16 + 6 + 15 = $\frac{37}{24}$. We then cancel this down: 37 ÷ 24 = 1 with a remainder of 13. Our answer is then expressed as $1\frac{13}{24}$.
4. Lowest common denominator = 16. $(\frac{15}{16} - \frac{4}{16}) = \frac{11}{16}$
5. Lowest common denominator = 24. $(\frac{21}{24} - \frac{16}{24}) = \frac{5}{24}$
6. Lowest common denominator = 21. $(\frac{18}{21} - \frac{7}{21}) = \frac{11}{21}$

When multiplying or dividing fractions – thank goodness – there is no need to find the lowest common denominator!

To multiply fractions you simply multiply the top figures together, then multiply the bottom figures together. Place the top result over the bottom result and cancel down if necessary. You can begin with some easy ones:

1. $\frac{1}{2} \times \frac{1}{4}$
2. $\frac{1}{3} \times \frac{1}{6}$

3. $\frac{1}{7} \times \frac{1}{3}$
4. $\frac{15}{16} \times \frac{3}{5}$

Answers

1. $\frac{1}{8}$
2. $\frac{1}{18}$
3. $\frac{1}{21}$
4. $\frac{45}{80}$ (cancels down to $\frac{9}{16}$)

To multiply mixed numbers, e.g. $1\frac{1}{4} \times \frac{7}{8}$, you must begin by converting the mixed number to a vulgar fraction. This means that it will be top heavy, but you must do this before you begin or you will get an incorrect result. Let's try both ways:

Method 1: $1\frac{1}{4} \times \frac{7}{8} = 1\frac{7}{32}$ *wrong*
Method 2: $\frac{5}{4} \times \frac{7}{8} = \frac{35}{32}$ (cancels down to $1\frac{3}{32}$)

Try the following:

1. $3\frac{1}{4} \times \frac{8}{9}$
2. $\frac{1}{16} \times 2\frac{1}{4}$
3. $4\frac{1}{2} \times \frac{1}{4}$

Answers

1. $\frac{13}{4} \times \frac{8}{9} = \frac{26}{9}$ (cancels down to $2\frac{8}{9}$)
2. $\frac{1}{16} \times \frac{9}{4} = \frac{9}{64}$
3. $\frac{9}{2} \times \frac{1}{4} = \frac{9}{8}$ (cancels down to $1\frac{1}{8}$)

Dividing fractions is where it gets really confusing! You leave the first fraction untouched and turn the second fraction on its head and multiply. Trust me, it really does work.

$\frac{1}{2} \div \frac{1}{4}$
$\frac{1}{2} \times \frac{4}{1} = \frac{4}{2}$ cancels to 2 – check it out on your calculator

Try the following:

1. $\frac{3}{5} \div \frac{5}{6}$
2. $\frac{1}{7} \div \frac{7}{8}$
3. $\frac{15}{16} \div \frac{1}{21}$

Answers

1. $\frac{3}{5} \times \frac{6}{5} = \frac{18}{25}$
2. $\frac{1}{7} \times \frac{8}{7} = \frac{8}{49}$
3. $\frac{15}{16} \times \frac{21}{1} = \frac{315}{16}$

Dealing with decimals

The position of the decimal point is crucial. The figure before the decimal point is a whole number and the figures after the decimal place represent a fraction. Decimals use base 10. The first figure after the decimal point is expressed as parts of 10, the second figure is expressed as parts of 100, the third as parts of 1000, etc.

$0.1 = \frac{1}{10}$ $0.01 = \frac{1}{100}$

$0.001 = \frac{1}{1000}$ $0.0001 = \frac{1}{10,000}$

$0.3 = \frac{3}{10}$ $0.05 = \frac{5}{100}\ (\frac{1}{20})$

$0.999 = \frac{999}{1000}$ $0.66 = \frac{66}{100}$

Always remember when adding or subtracting decimals to line the figures up on the decimal point, and you should get the correct result:

$$\begin{array}{rl} & 0.009 \\ + & 166.5 \\ + & 0.0008 \\ \hline & 166.5098 \end{array}$$

$$\begin{array}{rl} & 145.66 \\ - & 12.000076 \\ \hline & 133.659924 \end{array}$$

To multiply decimals, multiply the two numbers together and then put the decimal point in place by counting up the total number of figures *after* the decimal place.

```
   12.088        (3 numbers after decimal place
 ×  6.5          plus 1 number after decimal place equals 4,
   78.5720       so the decimal point in the answer is
                 placed 4 places from the right)
```

To divide decimals, ignore the decimal point and you will see that you get the same result.

5.55 ÷ 4.44 = 1.25

Now try these – ignore the decimal place and then check your results on a calculator first *with* the decimal places and then *without*:

6.55 ÷ 3.2 = 2.046875
17.2 ÷ 45.9 = 0.3747276 (to 7 decimal places)

This seems to be working very well, but what happens if we divide a decimal by a whole number, once again ignoring the decimal point?

26.75 ÷ 12 = 222.91666

This figure is clearly wrong. The correct answer should be 2.2291666. Remember when dividing decimals by whole numbers that you cannot ignore the decimal point!

Percentages and ratios

Percentages are very easy. Depending on whether we wish to find what percentage of a figure is represented by a number or what a certain percentage of a figure should be, the methods differ. Always remember that *per cent* is part of 100. Ratios do not need to be expressed in parts of 100. For example, if you have a 10% chance of catching a cold, you could say that you had one chance in ten, expressed as 1:10. We will look at ratios again in the section which deals with probability.

If you were asked to find 50% of a figure you could do it without thinking, but if you were asked to calculate VAT at 17.5% the method is the same.

1. Find 50% of £15

£15 multiplied by 50 (divided by 100)

$15 \times 50 = 750$

$\frac{750}{100} = £7.5$

2. Find 17.5% of £15

£15 multiplied by 17.5 (divided by 100)

$15 \times 17.5 = 262.5$

$\frac{262.5}{100} = £2.625$ (rounded to £2.63)

When you are told the figure and asked to find the percentage, the method is different:

1. What percentage of £15 does £12.25 represent?

£12.25 divided by £15 (being 100%) (multiplied by 100)

$12.25 \div 15 = 0.8166666$

$0.8166666 \times 100 = 81.66666\%$

It's time to test yourself. A small hotel needs to buy 5 pairs of sheets at £18.50 a pair, 5 pairs of pillow cases at £6.50 a pair, 10 feather pillows at £11.25 each, 1 tablecloth at £23.45 and 1 tablecloth at £17.00.

1. What is the total cost before VAT? If VAT is charged at 17.5%, what will be the total amount on the invoice?

2. The supplier says that if they pay the account within 7 days they can have a 5% discount on the prices. What will be the new total on the invoice? Remember to take the discount off *before* recalculating and adding the VAT.

5 pairs of sheets	@ £18.50 a pair	£92.50
5 pillow cases	@ £6.50 a pair	£32.50
10 pillows	@ £11.25 each	£112.50

1 tablecloth	@ £23.45	£23.45
1 tablecloth	@ £17.00	£17.00

Answers

1. Total without VAT — £277.95
   VAT — £48.64
   Invoice total — £326.59

2. Total without VAT — £277.95
   Less 5% discount — £13.89
   Revised total without VAT — £264.06
   VAT — £46.21
   New invoice total — £310.27

Here are two simple problems. Try *estimating* the results before you either work them out manually or use a calculator. See how close you got.

1. If I go shopping with £20, how much change should I expect if I buy:

2.5kg of cheese at £4.80 per kg, 1 loaf of bread at £0.68, 0.50kg of bacon at £5.00 per kg and a 4-litre carton of milk at £0.30 per litre?

2. I have a twin brother and for our birthday we received money from all our aunts and uncles. How much money could we each expect if we share it evenly?

Aunt Mildred gave £15.00, Aunt Mary Ann gave £25, Aunt Valerie gave £12 and Uncle Fred gave £44.50.

Answers

1. £3.62 change from £20
2. Each twin received £48.25

Probability

Probability is far from an exact science and my advice to you is never to gamble!

If we take the example of a coin, providing it is normal and one side has a head and the other a tail, then the chances of it landing 'head' side up are in the ratio of 50:50, i.e. 1 in 2. Of course, the chances of it landing 'tail' side up are also 1 in 2.

You might think that your coin would conveniently land one side up and then the other, but unfortunately this is not the case. Each time you toss your coin there is still a 50:50 chance.

If we turn our attention to throwing a dice, instead of there being two possibilities, there are six. I need to throw a 6 to win a game, so what are my chances?

1 in 6.

Playing cards are even more difficult to predict, since there are 52 cards in a pack. So, if I nominate one card, say the Jack of Diamonds, I have only a 1 in 52 chance of selecting the right card.

If I am prepared to settle for any diamond, then the odds get much better. Since there are 13 diamonds in a pack, I now have a 13 in 52 chance of success.

Shapes and sizes

All shapes with four sides are quadrilaterals. They have other names, depending on the shape:

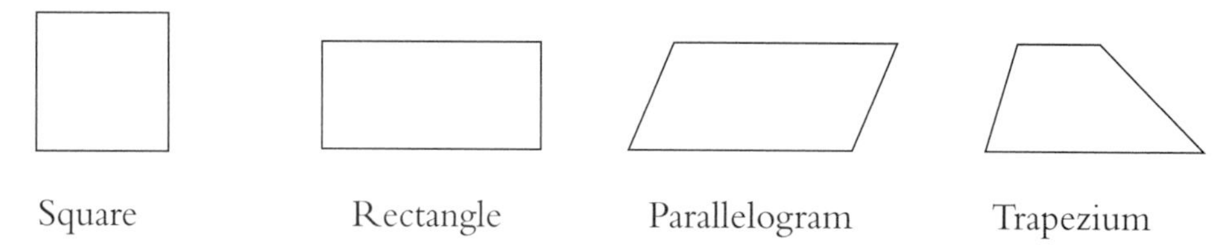

Square Rectangle Parallelogram Trapezium

With so many different shapes, how many degrees do they have? In fact, each of these shapes, because they have four sides, has the same number of degrees – 360.

A triangle has 180°. A pentagon (5 sides) has 520°. It is easy to find how many degrees any shape has: the number of sides less 2 multiplied by 180.

Perimeters and areas

The perimeter is the outside of a shape. To find the perimeter, you simply measure the length of each of the sides and add them together. So if I have a quadrilateral which measures 1.5m + 1.5m + 1.5m + 1.5m, then the perimeter will be 6m.

Areas can be more difficult to find, especially if you are dealing with an odd shape. We will begin with a nice easy square:

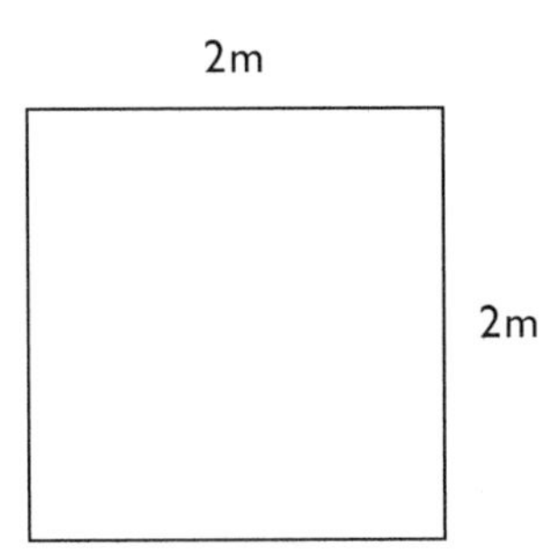

Area = base × height: $2\text{m} \times 2\text{m} = 4\text{m}^2$

Let's try something a bit more challenging:

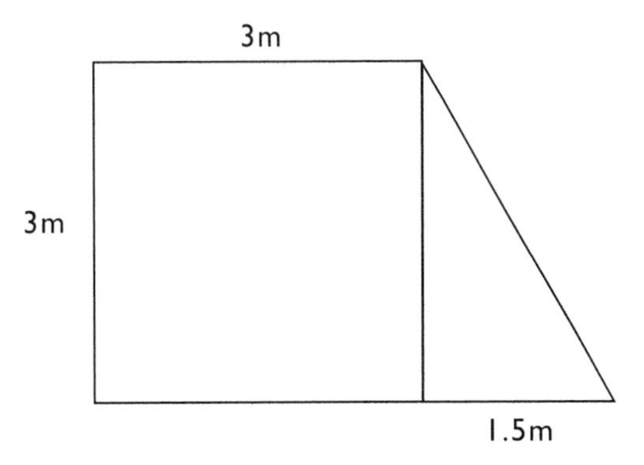

The square section is easy: $3\text{m} \times 3\text{m} = 9\text{m}^2$

We can see that the base measurement of the triangular section measures 1.5m, and we know that the height is 3m.

We say that the area of a triangle is ½ base multiplied by the height: $\frac{1}{2} \times 1.5 \times 3 = 2.25\text{m}^2$

To find the total area we now simply add the area of the square section to that of the triangular section:

$9\text{m}^2 + 2.25\text{m}^2 = 11.25\text{m}^2$

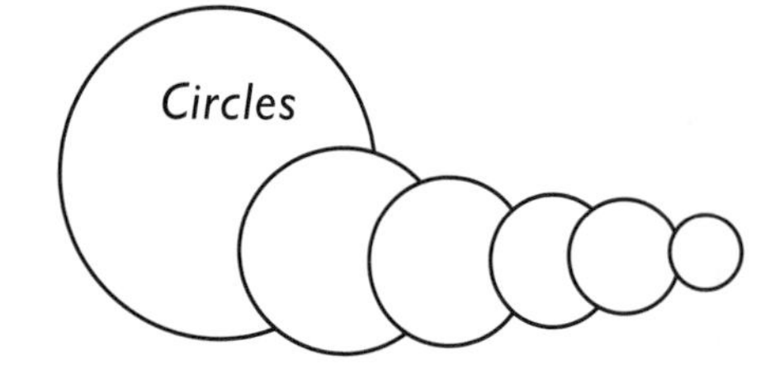

Circles are tricky things. They have no base or height and so a whole new set of rules needs to be applied. We need to discover the radius, the diameter and the circumference. The radius is taken from the centre point of the circle, out to the edge. The diameter is the line from edge to edge of the circle, passing through the centre. The diameter is, therefore, twice the radius. The circumference (the outside edge of the circle; the perimeter) is calculated using pi, and the symbol for this is π. Pi is a Greek letter and is the same for all circles. Its value cannot be stated exactly so an approximate figure of 3.142, or $^{22}/_{7}$, is used.

Before we begin our calculations, we apply letters to shorten the formula:

c = circumference	r = radius
d = diameter	a = area

The formula for finding c is:

Another method of expressing c is:

We will work through one easy example. Find the circumference of a circle with a diameter of 10m (the answer will be reduced to 2 decimal places):

$c = 10\,\pi = 31.42$m

If the radius only is known, then the formula would be $c = 2\pi \times 5 = 31.42$.

Try the following – you can use your calculator if you really need to. If you do not have a scientific calculator simply use the value of pi.

1. Find the circumference of a circle with a radius of 22m.
2. Find the circumference of a circle with a radius of 72m.
3. Find the circumference of a circle with a diameter of 48cm.
4. Find the circumference of a circle with a diameter of 96cm.

Answers

1. 138.248m
2. 452.448m

3. 150.816cm
4. 301.632cm

To find the area of a circle we need to use *pi* once again. This time the formula is

$a = \pi \times r \times r = \pi r^2$

To find the area of a circle with a radius of 4cm:

$a = \pi 4^2 = 16\ \pi = 50.27cm^2$

Try the following exercises:

1. Find the area of a circle whose radius is 2cm.
2. Find the area of a circle whose radius is 3cm.
3. Find the area of a circle whose radius is 12cm.

To find the area of a circle when you know the diameter, use πr^2.

To use this formula it is first necessary to find the radius ($\frac{d}{2}$).

4. Find the area of a circle whose diameter is 6cm.
5. Find the area of a circle whose diameter is 32cm.
6. Find the area of a circle whose diameter is 42cm.

To find the area of a semi-circle, the formula is $\frac{\pi r^2}{2}$.

Answers

1. $12.586cm^2$
2. $28.278cm^2$
3. $452.448cm^2$
4. $28.278cm^2$
5. $804.352cm^2$
6. $1385.622cm^2$

Averages

What is an average? When people talk about averages, they are normally referring to the *mean* average. In fact, two other averages are commonly used, known as *median* and *mode*.

Definition:

The *median* is the mid range of a group of figures.
The *mode* is the figure that appears most frequently, the 'fashion'.
The *mean* average is a calculated average.

The best way to explain how these work is to look at an example. In a survey, 21 boys, aged 12, were asked for their sports shoe sizes and the following data were collected:

SIZE	TALLY	FREQUENCY
5	I	1
5.5	II	2
6	III	3
6.5	III	3
7	IIII	4
7.5	II	2
8	I	1
8.5	I	1
9	II	2
9.5	I	1
10	I	1

The mode average is size 7. In order to find the median average, it is necessary to place each shoe size in ascending order, in line. Remember that although there are only 11 different shoe sizes, you need to take the frequency into account or your answer will be incorrect:

5 5.5 5.5 6 6 6 6.5 6.5 6.5 7 $\underline{7}$ 7 7 7.5 7.5 8 8.5 9 9 9.5 10

The median average is also 7.

The mean average is found by adding up *all* the shoe sizes and then dividing by the total frequency of 21.

The total of all the shoe sizes is 150.5. The mean average is 150.5 ÷ 21 = 7.166 (limited to 3 decimal places).

You will notice that the mean average has given us a slightly different, more accurate result. However, if this information was required by a sports shoe manufacturer, the mode average would be by far the most useful.

Using charts and graphs to highlight your findings

Deciding on the type of graph that is most suitable can be confusing. Unless you choose wisely, your graph may not indicate clearly what you are hoping to show.

Pie charts

This is a simple way of displaying a single range of data and it is normally one of the first types of graph that we are introduced to as children. A typical problem given to very young children to solve might be:

James and David have 12 sweets. If they share them equally how many do they each have? Draw a pie chart to show your findings.

James has six sweets and David has six sweets. The chart would be roughly drawn as shown below. The child would be encouraged to give the chart a heading so that the reader knew its purpose, and write James and David's names and what percentage of sweets each of them had.

Chart to show how 12 sweets were shared equally.

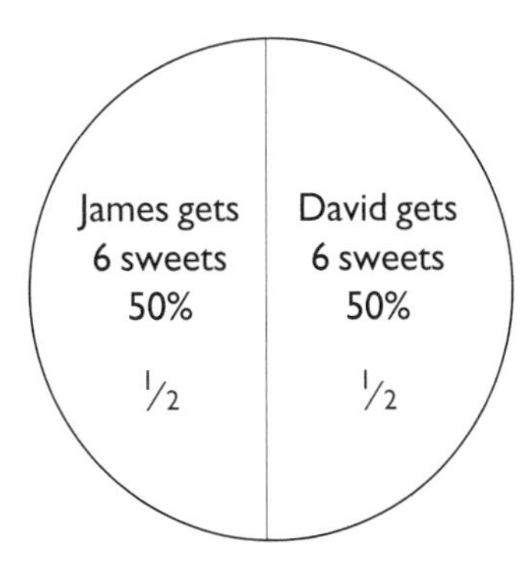

As children get older, they are taught to draw pie charts more accurately by dividing the chart up into the exact number of degrees represented by the data.

A circle has 360° and so to chart the results correctly you will need to find how these degrees need to be shared.

360° represent 100%, i.e. for each 1% there are 3.6°

If we take an example, we can then work through it to see how we can hand draw an accurate pie chart.

£20.00 is shared as follows: Damien gets £3.00, Clive gets £2.00, Ranjit and Tony each get £2.50, Claire gets £3.00, Anne gets £2.50, Tanya gets £1.50 and David gets £3.

We begin by finding what percentage of the £20 each child gets.

Reminder of method: each share of the £20 is divided by 20 and the result is then multiplied by 100.

$$\frac{£3}{£20} \times 100 = 15\%$$

$$\frac{£2}{£20} \times 100 = 10\%$$

$$\frac{£2.50}{£20} \times 100 = 12.5\%$$

$$\frac{£1.50}{£20} \times 100 = 7.5\%$$

CHILD	PERCENTAGE	DEGREES
Damien	15%	54°
Clive	10%	36°
Ranjit	12.5%	45°
Tony	12.5%	45°
Claire	15%	54°
Anne	12.5%	45°
Tanya	7.5%	27°
David	15%	54°

Now you have all your calculations you can draw your circle using a compass and find how to divide the circle up correctly by using a protractor. Alternatively, you could load a computerized spreadsheet package, enter the data and let the computer do all the hard work for you!

Line graphs

A simple line graph could be used to record an athlete's pulse rate at different points during the day. In a line graph, the points at which data appear are joined together with a simple line.

Another type of line graph which is commonly used is an XY line graph (see Figure 2.2). This type of graph is used when two or more sets of data need to

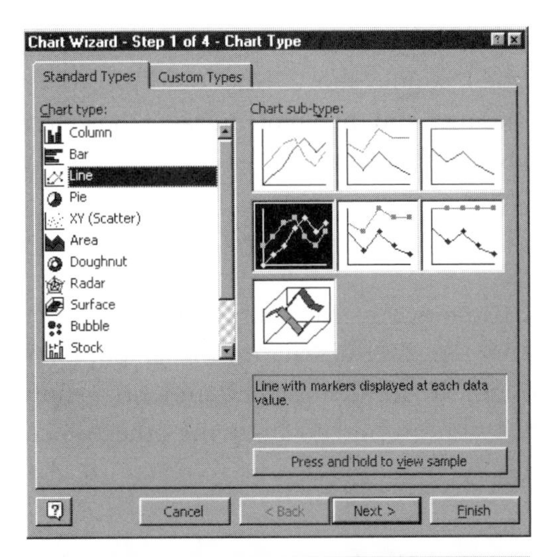

Figure 2.2 Line graph

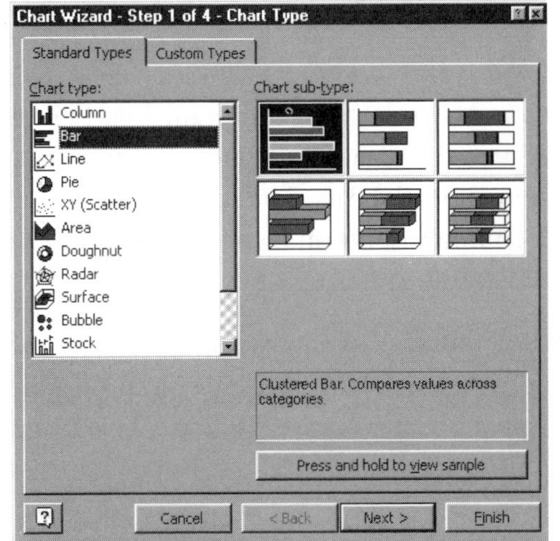

Figure 2.3 Bar chart

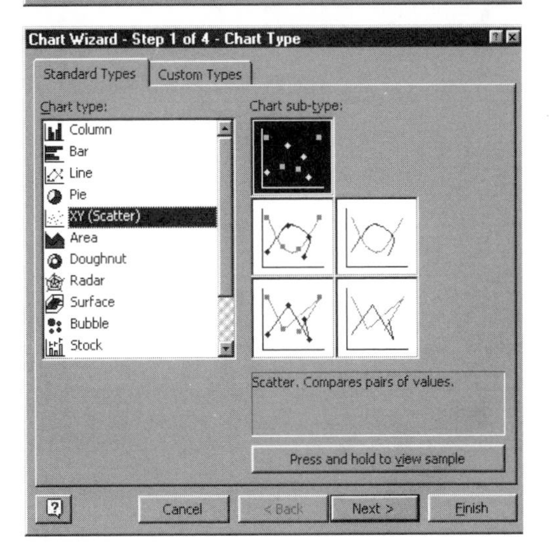

Figure 2.4 Scattergram

be represented. For example, to take the example above, you could record an athlete's pulse rate and temperature at set times, and then plot and label the graph using different colours for the pulse rate and temperature.

Bar charts

If you were asked to plot students' test results, you could use a bar chart (see Figure 2.3). Rather than lines indicating the level of data on the graph, solid 'bars' of colour or shading are used to indicate the results. The students' names would go along one axis while their test scores would go along the other. Once the chart is labelled, the results of each student should be easy to recognize at a glance.

Scattergrams

Where you have widely spread data, you may select a scattergram (see Figure 2.4) to show the distribution of data. Since the data are so widely distributed, neither lines nor columns could accurately show the data. The data would appear as dots or small crosses on the graph. A common solution is to then find the *line of best fit* by drawing a line through the densest gathering of data.

The question of graphs could fill a whole book. You can, with trial and error, teach yourself the best charts and graphs to use, or do some research of your own. Try looking at a computerized spreadsheet software package. The range and types of graph available are excellent.

3

Information Technology Core Skills

Elements and Performance Criteria relating to Information Technology

We will begin by looking at how you can provide this evidence.

1 Prepare information

1.1 *Select information appropriate to the task*

This will be done naturally. Whatever the assignment you are working on, you will need to do some research. This may be partly from theory learned in class, from class handouts, from books, journals, etc., or from the Internet. This information may include text, graphics and numbers.

- A good way of providing proof is to provide a bibliography, detailing the source of your information, e.g. name of article or book, author and publisher and possibly page number(s).

1.2 *Enter information into software in ways that will make it easy to edit*

Once again, this will be done naturally. All computer application software is designed to make editing very easy. As you work through your assignments you will proofread your work and make corrections as and when necessary, and of course you will use the spell checker and grammar checker.

You will save at very regular intervals – we will discuss at a later stage why this is so essential.

You can use manuals or classroom handouts to aid you in using the various software packages.

If, during the course of your work, you find that there is a fault in the system, you can, *with the permission of your tutor*, try to rectify the problem.

- Your IT tutor should observe you entering and editing your work. He/she may make a note of the fact that you have achieved this Performance Criterion. You might like to ask him/her to provide you with a signature as proof.

1.3 *Keep source information required for the task*

Simply retain a copy of the information. This may be in note form or a photocopy of material used.

1.4 *Store input systematically and make back-up copies*

Save your work as you go! There is nothing worse than working for hours on a project, only to see it disappear when the computer system fails. In addition to saving your work regularly, it is advisable to make a back-up of your file on another floppy disk. If you lose one, or it becomes corrupted in some way, you will always have the second copy to fall back on.

It is important that you learn how the computer works. We will cover this at a later stage.

- Show your lecturer the directory on your disk so that he/she can confirm that you have saved work and made a back-up.

1.5 *Configure software to aid input of information*

All software comes with *default settings*. This simply means that unless you change these settings your work will be in a standard font, of a standard size, with standard layout, line spacing, margins and tab stops. You should adjust these settings in a way which will allow for the most suitable format. We will be looking at how to do this.

- Once again, ask your lecturer to observe you making changes. These changes will become evident when you print out your work, so there will be two types of evidence.

2 Process information

2.1 *Find information required for the task*

In order to process the information input during the preparation stage, you will access relevant files by searching directories for specific file names. Another means by which you can find the information required is by searching a file, e.g. a database file, to match a specific criterion. You will also access remote sites in order to find suitable information. This can be done by 'downloading' information from a file server or possibly from the World Wide Web of the Internet.

- Once again, in order to provide proof that you have managed this task, ask your tutor to observe you or include a full bibliography.

2.2 *Use appropriate software to edit information*

This will be achieved when you load the application software used during the preparation stage. Whether you are using a word processing package, spreadsheet package, or database package, editing of text, numbers and graphics is easy.

It should be remembered that, providing the different types of application software used are compatible, it should be possible to integrate all your work into a single document, e.g. a report. This will give the added benefit of providing a uniform format for the whole of your project. Editing involves amending, moving, reformatting, copying, deleting, inserting, etc.

- An obvious method of providing proof that you have edited information is to retain a printout of your original work for comparison with the final version.

2.3 *Process numeric information by using software to make calculations*

The most effective way of achieving this Performance Criterion is to use a spreadsheet package, as this gives by far the greatest flexibility. By creating columns and rows holding data, it is possible to carry out calculations, from the most basic to very complex equations. Look at the section for spreadsheets to see just how easy it is.

- Evidence can be provided by supplying a printout of your work showing the formulae used.

2.4 *Reorganize information as required for the task*

This Performance Criterion can be achieved by sorting stored data in tables, columns or database files.

- Evidence is easily provided by supplying printouts of files, before and after sorting or restructuring.

2.5 *Save work at appropriate intervals*

When is it appropriate to save work? Obviously before and after changes are made and when the final version has been completed, but also at regular intervals: it is recommended that you save every 20 minutes or so. This may not appear necessary, but if the computer experiences a problem you could lose your work.

- Your tutor may like to observe you saving your work or you could provide a list of files in your directory with dates/times.

2.6 *Combine information from different sources, resolving differences of format*

This will be achieved by inserting files into other files, either using the same application software or some other suitable package. Examples of how to do this will be given in the final section, concerning assignments.

- Evidence will be in the form of separate printouts of documents and one printout showing the work once it has been fully integrated.

2.7 *Create automated routines that aid efficient processing of information*

Automated routines save time and can ensure that all your work is in a uniform format. We will look at achieving this Performance Criterion by using *macros*. You can 'record' macros by selecting settings for your own format. Once the macro has been saved and stored, you only need to use the macro in order to reproduce all the settings automatically.

- In order to gain the necessary evidence, ask your tutor to observe you recording and using macros.

3 Present information

3.1 *Prepare information for presentation*

The professional presentation of work is vital. Poorly presented work will lose you marks. If you have put a lot of effort into research for your assignment or project, the whole effect can be spoiled if the final project is badly presented.

This involves the planning and preparing of the format to meet the requirements of the task. Work should be dated and pages numbered. As your work progresses, you should save different versions.

- If you have produced a rough plan or outline for the work, this should be submitted as evidence of preparation.

3.2 *Present information in different ways and select which way best meets the requirements of the task*

This Performance Criterion leads naturally on from the preparation for presentation stage. A lot of effort should be put into deciding on the most suitable format for the work. For example, if you have to give a presentation to the class, rather than simply submit a paper-based assignment, the methods chosen will be very different.

- Evidence for this Performance Criterion will be in the form of observation and the final printed project.

3.3 *Use appropriate software to display information*

This would seem to be very obvious, but many people make mistakes. It is possible to use a word processing package to create posters, but you would be far better using a desktop publishing package. Calculations can be carried out in some word processing packages and/or database packages, but sums are far better done by using a spreadsheet package.

If you need to give a presentation to the class, you should use a specialized package such as Microsoft Powerpoint, as this gives you far greater control over the presentation and you can time slides and even record sound if you wish.

- The evidence that this Performance Criterion has been achieved will be self evident when you give the presentation and/or submit your project.

3.4 *Use appropriate software to produce hard copies of information*

Whatever the application software chosen, you should be able to select the most suitable printer for the purpose. For example, if you are giving a class presentation, use of a colour printer can give added interest.

The better the quality of print you can manage, the more effective the final product will be.

- Evidence will be proved by the quality of the project and/or class handouts you submit. If you do not have access to good quality printers, your lecturer should take this into account and not penalize you.

3.5 *Present combined information in a consistent format*

If you have processed your assignments/projects by integrating files together and readjusting the format so that it is uniform, you will have already gained this Performance Criterion.

- Evidence will be proven by the hard copy of the final project.

3.6 *Store information in files and make back-up copies*

Save your work systematically as you go, ensuring each version is saved and backing-up files by copying to another disk.

- By your lecturer observing the contents of your disk directories you can provide evidence that this Performance Criterion has been achieved.

4 Evaluate the use of Information Technology

Evaluation of each assignment is a requirement of GNVQ, but the evaluation referred to in this Performance Criterion should be specific to the Information Technology used in the assignment and will relate to your research, presentation and delivery of the final assignment.

You should state *how* you have used Information Technology and the benefits and limitations (if any).

This is one Core Skill element that might be best tackled by writing a separate report. It only needs to be done in any great depth once and should relate to one specific assignment.

An example of how you can achieve this Performance Criterion will be given in the final section, when we look at sample assignments.

- Evidence will be in the form of a report.

4

Theory and Practice in Information Technology

Introduction to word processing

The following chapters will take you through some of the functions of word processing and show you ideas on formatting documents. No matter how much effort you have put into planning and researching your assignment, it could all be spoilt if you don't learn to make the most of what the word processor has to offer.

There are many different word processing software packages and it is impossible to give specific instructions for every user. For this reason, we will choose the most popular package on the market at the present time (Microsoft Word) to give instruction. Whatever package *you* are using, you will be able to obtain the same results by giving slightly different instructions.

When you first select Microsoft Word, you will notice that there are various words and icons at the top of the screen (see Figure 4.1).

Each of the following has a 'drop down menu'. This simply means that if you click on any of these words a list appears, from which you will be able to select the relevant option:

File, Edit, View, Insert, Format, Tools, Table, Window and Help

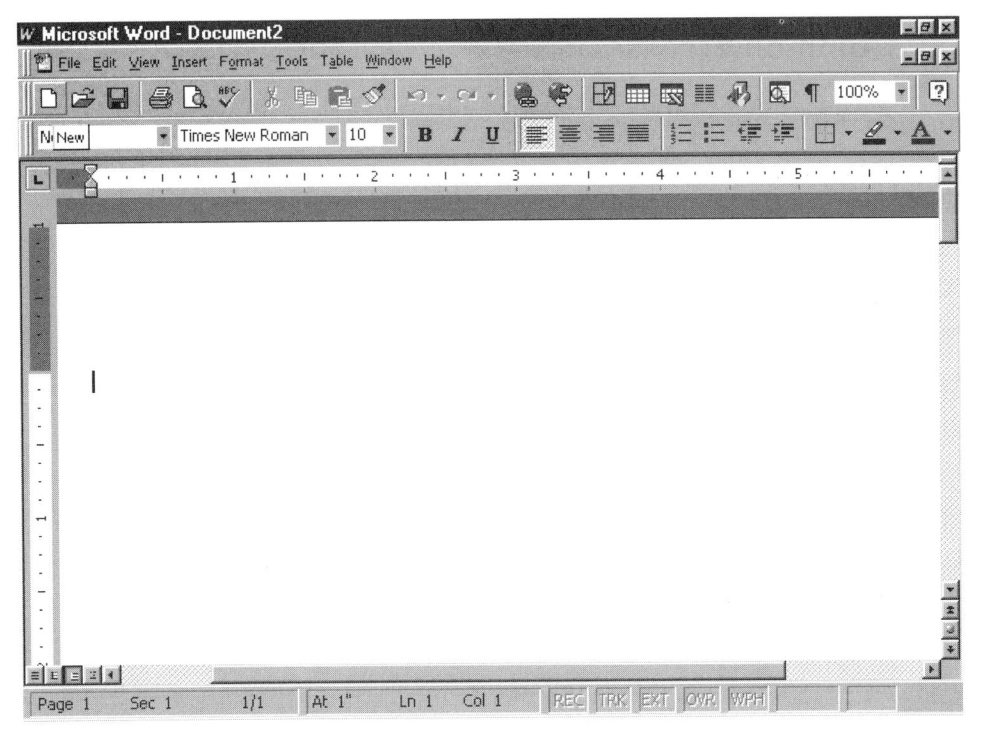

Figure 4.1 Microsoft Word screen

To find out what the icons represent and how they can help you, simply move your mouse so that the cursor is on the icon and a written description will be displayed below the icon.

Whatever the format you decide upon, there are certain standards that should be maintained. The same rules apply when word processing as with writing, e.g. a capital letter for the beginning of each new sentence and also for proper nouns.

Always use correct spacing after punctuation, i.e. one space after a comma, colon or semicolon. The RSA (Royal Society of Arts) Examination Board used to insist on two spaces after full stops, question marks and exclamation marks, but it is now permitted to use either one or two spaces.

Leave one clear line space between paragraphs, i.e. press the return (enter) key twice.

Common errors

What is wrong with the following sentence?

> As a result of this survey it was found that alot of air travellers were late checking in.

The first glaring error is that no space has been left between *a* and *lot*. There is no such word, as the spell checker will tell you. It may suggest *allot*, which means to share.

Even if you do leave the correct space, making the sentence read *As a result of this survey it was found that a lot of air travellers were late checking in*, the second error must be recognized. Just what is 'a lot'? Your idea of a lot of patients will be different from mine. Always be as precise as possible, especially when giving statistics.

The revised sentence might look like this:

> As a result of this survey concerning air travel it was found that 52% of air travellers were late checking in.

Choosing the correct layout

A number of exercises are included in this section. Key in these exercises as shown and then make adjustments. You should see what an improvement can be made. Use default settings. (Default settings are standard settings in the software for margins, line spacing, and font type and size.)

Exercise 1

Centring and emboldening text, changing to upper case, spacing, inserting and splitting paragraphs

- Key in the following text:

Why do I need to use the computer?

Whatever branch of the leisure industry you choose, you will need to be able to use computers.Computers are now in leisure centres,restaurants,travel agents and airports.For example if we think of a leisure centre,a computer can be used to help book clients in to use sports facilities and this should avoid double booking.The centre can also have a database with all members' details so that letters can be sent when their membership has expired.

- Save your work by selecting the correct drive and giving a suitable file name. Print one copy and close the file.
- Now re-open the file and edit to make the following corrections:

  1. Centre and embolden the heading and change the format to use capital letters.
  2. Go through the work and use the correct spacing after punctuation.
  3. Make a new paragraph of the sentence beginning *For example...* by pressing the return (enter) key twice.
  4. Insert the word 'computerized' before 'database' in the sentence beginning *The centre can also have a database.*

The result should look like this:

WHY DO I NEED TO USE THE COMPUTER?

Whatever branch of the leisure industry you choose, you will need to be able to use computers. Computers are now in leisure centres, restaurants, travel agents and airports.

For example if we think of a leisure centre, a computer can be used to help book clients in to use sports facilities and this should avoid double booking. The centre can also have a computerized database with all members' details so that letters can be sent when their membership has expired.

Exercise 2

Using graphics

Task Design a menu for a small family restaurant

The menu should be well laid out and contain at least one suitable graphic. Most word processing packages have *Clip Art*. (Select the Picture option from the Insert menu.) Go through the list and find something suitable for the type of restaurant. Vary the size and style of font and make use of emboldening and centring to improve the appearance.

Some ideas are contained within the sample shown in Figure 4.2.

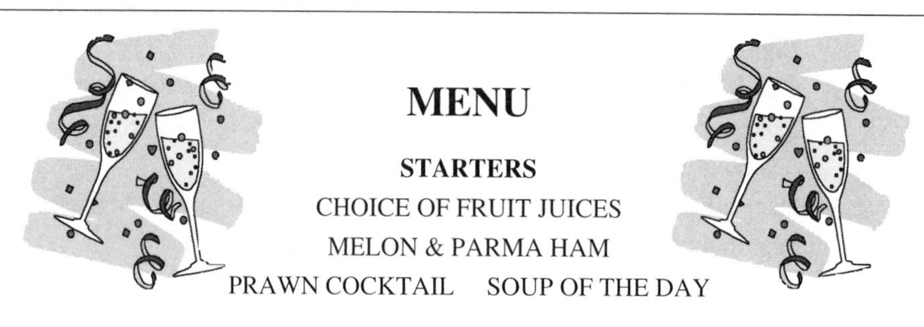

MENU

STARTERS

CHOICE OF FRUIT JUICES

MELON & PARMA HAM

PRAWN COCKTAIL SOUP OF THE DAY

MAIN COURSE

DOVER SOLE GRILLED SEA BASS

ROAST SCOTTISH BEEF SADDLE OF LAMB

CHOICE OF VEGETARIAN DISHES AVAILABLE

CHOICE OF ROAST, NEW OR JACKET POTATOES

FRESH VEGETABLES OR SELECTION FROM THE SALAD BAR

SWEETS

CREME CARAMEL APPLE STRUDEL

BLACK FOREST GATEAU

SERVED WITH CREAM OR ICE CREAM

SELECTION OF CHEESES AND CRACKERS

COFFEE AND MINTS

A WIDE SELECTION OF WINES AND LIQUEURS

Figure 4.2 Sample menu

Exercise 3

Editing and inserting text and linking paragraphs

Key in the following using default settings:

COMPUTERS IN THE TRAVEL INDUSTRY

Thanks to computers, life has been made much easier for travel agents. They are able to check on availability of flights and/or holidays by accessing a specialized travel database. In order to be able to do this their computers must have the correct communications link.

This is obviously a great improvement on using the telephone to see what flights and hotels are available for a particular date.

Television viewers are also able to check on holiday bargains if they have Teletext on their television at home. Special pages are prepared giving details of holiday availability, and these are updated regularly in order to give the latest position to the user. A great deal of other information can be obtained from Teletext including weather forecasts all over the world and the latest exchange rates.

Tasks

1. Proofread and spell check your work.
2. Print and save to floppy disk as EX2.
3. Close the file.
4. Retrieve the document by opening EX2.
5. Centre and embolden the heading and change the style and size of font.
6. Set the right and left margins to 1.5 inches and the top and bottom margins to 2.5 inches.
7. Amend the sentence beginning *This is obviously a great improvement on using the telephone ...* to read *This is obviously a great improvement on using the telephone to get through to each individual airline or hotel to check on availability of flights and/or hotels.*
8. Join the paragraph beginning *This is obviously a great improvement....* to the paragraph ending *communications link.* (Method: position the cursor in front of the *T* of *This* and delete spaces to the left until the

paragraphs are joined and there is a suitable gap between the sentences.)

9. Insert the word *currency* before *exchange rates*, ensuring there is one space before and one after the word.
10. Check through your work, spell check and view the page before printing.
11. Save your work as EX2B, keeping the original document intact.

The result should look like this:

COMPUTERS IN THE TRAVEL INDUSTRY

Thanks to computers, life has been made much easier for travel agents. They are able to check on availability of flights and/or holidays by accessing a specialized travel database. In order to be able to do this their computers must have the correct communications link. This is obviously a great improvement on using the telephone to get through to each individual airline or hotel to check on availability of flights and/or hotels.

Television viewers are also able to check on holiday bargains if they have Teletext on their television at home. Special pages are prepared giving details of holiday availability, and these are updated regularly in order to give the latest position to the user. A great deal of other information can be obtained from Teletext including weather forecasts all over the world and the latest currency exchange rates.

Exercise 4

Further editing

- **Key in the following using default settings:**

NUTRITIONAL SUPPLEMENTS AND ATHLETICS

81 per cent of Olympic athletes regularly use nutritional supplements to improve their performance. The body's need for some vitamins and minerals increases when you exercise a lot.

VITAMIN B1 is excellent at fighting fatigue and is commonly used by marathon runners.

VITAMINS B3 AND B12 also work in synergy with Vitamin B1.

Vitamin B3 helps the body to burn its free fats as energy; this benefits oxygen metabolism and should increase the production of adrenaline during exercise.

To be really effective, any supplements taken to improve performance need to be supported by a whole range of nutrients including vitamin A, the full range of B vitamins, vitamins E and D.

WARNING! NEVER EXCEED THE RECOMMENDED DOSE WHEN TAKING ANY SUPPLEMENTS. SOME VITAMINS SUCH AS VITAMIN C ARE NOT STORED BY THE BODY BUT OTHER VITAMINS ARE STORED BY THE BODY AND A BUILD-UP OF THESE CAN BE DANGEROUS.

Tasks

1. Proofread your work.
2. Spell check and grammar check your work.
3. Make any necessary corrections before saving.
4. Print a single copy of the document.
5. Retrieve the file and make the following modifications:

   - Centre and embolden heading.
   - Delete the words *per cent* and replace them with the percentage symbol %.
   - Replace the word *synergy* in paragraph 3 and replace it with *harmony*.
   - Add a final sentence to the end of paragraph 4: *A regular intake of Vitamin C promotes healing and enables the body to take up iron. This vitamin is also extensively used in cases of anaemia.*
   - Use the spell check and, if correct, print a copy of the revised document.
   - Save your work by overwriting the original file, i.e. saving under the same file name as before.

See page 46 for the result.

NUTRITIONAL SUPPLEMENTS AND ATHLETICS

81% of Olympic athletes regularly use nutritional supplements to improve their performance. The body's need for some vitamins and minerals increases when you exercise a lot.

VITAMIN B1 is excellent at fighting fatigue and is commonly used by marathon runners.

VITAMINS B3 AND B12 also work in harmony with Vitamin B1.

Vitamin B3 helps the body to burn its free fats as energy; this benefits oxygen metabolism and should increase the production of adrenaline during exercise. A regular intake of Vitamin C promotes healing and enables the body to take up iron. This vitamin is also extensively used in cases of anaemia.

To be really effective, any supplements taken to improve performance need to be supported by a whole range of nutrients including vitamin A, the full range of B vitamins, vitamins E and D.

WARNING! NEVER EXCEED THE RECOMMENDED DOSE WHEN TAKING ANY SUPPLEMENTS. SOME VITAMINS SUCH AS VITAMIN C ARE NOT STORED BY THE BODY BUT OTHER VITAMINS ARE STORED BY THE BODY AND A BUILD-UP OF THESE CAN BE DANGEROUS.

Exercise 5

Making a poster

Task Design a poster suitable for advertising cruises in Alaska

- Select a suitable graphic – you may either use Clip Art or scan in a picture of your own. A sample is shown in Figure 4.3.

Figure 4.3 Poster advertising cruises

Exercise 6

Inserting files

- Key in the following using default settings:

Whether you book your holiday early or wait for a last minute special offer will depend on how flexible you are. If you have set your heart on a particular hotel in a particular resort you must book your holiday in plenty of time. People who book early are sometimes rewarded with some kind of special deal, e.g. free places for children or perhaps free holiday insurance.

If you aren't too bothered about the resort or type of accommodation, then you can pick up some real last minute bargains. You will be able to tell all your fellow holiday-makers about the excellent deal you got – this is not, however, likely to make you many friends!

- Save your work and call the file *Addition*. Close the document.
- Begin a new document and key in the following:

BOOKING YOUR HOLIDAYS

There are many decisions that will influence the way in which you book your holiday. You may use a travel agent and select a package holiday. Alternatively, you may want to be free from the constraints of a package deal where everything is organized for you. On the whole, package holidays work out cheaper than taking a charter flight and making your own arrangements for accommodation.

Whatever your holiday destination, in order to get the most from your holiday you must ensure that you look after your health. Diarrhoea and sickness are the most common complaints among holiday-makers.

Tasks

1. Save your document as *Holiday*. Do not close the file.
2. Leave the file displayed on the screen and position the cursor on the W of Whatever your holiday... .

3. Now select the *Insert* option from the toolbar and select the *insert file* option. A list of stored files will be displayed. Select the file called *Addition.*
4. You have now joined two files together to form a single document. Adjust the line spacing by pressing the enter key. The final paragraph should now begin: 'Whatever your holiday destination…'.

The result should look like this:

BOOKING YOUR HOLIDAYS

There are many decisions that will influence the way in which you book your holiday. You may use a travel agent and select a package holiday. Alternatively, you may want to be free from the constraints of a package deal where everything is organized for you. On the whole, package holidays work out cheaper than taking a charter flight and making your own arrangements for accommodation.

Whether you book your holiday early or wait for a last minute special offer will depend on how flexible you are. If you have set your heart on a particular hotel in a particular resort you must book your holiday in plenty of time. People who book early are sometimes rewarded with some kind of special deal, e.g. free places for children or perhaps free holiday insurance.

If you aren't too bothered about the resort or type of accommodation, then you can pick up some real last minute bargains. You will be able to tell all your fellow holiday-makers about the excellent deal you got – this is not, however, likely to make you many friends!

Whatever your holiday destination, in order to get the most from your holiday you must ensure that you look after your health. Diarrhoea and sickness are the most common complaints among holiday-makers.

Exercise 7

Cutting and pasting, changing margins

- Type the following using default settings:

THE LEISURE INDUSTRY

More and more leisure centres have sprung up in the United Kingdom. There are a number of reasons for this: This pattern has been repeated in most other affluent countries.

Our society as a whole is more affluent than it once was.

People take more of an interest in health and fitness.

Generally speaking people now work shorter hours.

People make better use of spare time.

Stressed executives often play sport to relieve tension.

People are now living longer thanks partly to medical breakthroughs and improved diets and exercise regimes. It is not unusual to see quite old people successfully taking part in marathons these days.

Tasks

- Save your document and print a copy. Open the file and adjust as follows:

1. Centre and embolden the heading.
2. Cut the phrase *This pattern has been repeated in most other affluent countries.* Paste it so that it comes before *There are a number of reasons for this:*. Adjust the spacing as necessary.
3. Bullet each of the points and adjust the spacing as necessary.
4. Put a footer on the document – this should include your name and the current date but no page number.
5. Change the margins to 1.5" on both the left and right hand sides.
6. Save and print the revised document.

The final result should look like this:

THE LEISURE INDUSTRY

More and more leisure centres have sprung up in the United Kingdom. This pattern has been repeated in most other affluent countries. There are a number of reasons for this:

- Our society as a whole is more affluent than it once was.
- People take more of an interest in health and fitness.
- Generally speaking people now work shorter hours.
- People make better use of spare time.
- Stressed executives often play sport to relieve tension.

People are now living longer thanks partly to medical breakthroughs and improved diets and exercise regimes. It is not unusual to see quite old people successfully taking part in marathons these days.

Exercise 8

Letter layout

Important – no matter how good a personality you have, this alone will not get you an interview. Your first point of contact will normally be a letter and curriculum vitae or personal profile – so make them impressive!

Task

- Write a letter in the format shown on page 52, introducing yourself and asking whether the organization has any vacancies. Try the example shown and then modify it until you feel it is right for you.

Note: *Always* proofread and spell check your work!

19 Garland Street
CHICHESTER
West Sussex
PO21 9JJ
(today's date in the following format) 6 June 1999

Mr J. Fenchurch
Personnel Manager
Tourist Information Centre
South Street
CHICHESTER
West Sussex
PO20 8JG

Dear Mr Fenchurch

I would like to introduce myself. My name is Daniel Stewart and I am a student at Chichester Sixth Form College. I am nearing completion of a two-year full-time BTEC GNVQ Advanced Level course in Leisure and Tourism, and I intend to make my career in tourism. I would really like to hear from you if you have any suitable vacancies either now or in the near future.

I enclose a copy of my curriculum vitae, giving details of my qualifications and experience to date and hope that this will be of interest.

An important part of the GNVQ course is work experience. During the course of my studies I had a two-week placement at a tourist information centre in Surrey. I very much enjoyed the time I spent there and felt that it gave me a good insight into the day-to-day running of the centre.

As you will see from my CV, I have had a part-time job working on the reception desk of a local leisure centre and very much enjoy meeting and helping members of the public. I feel that this experience will make me a suitable candidate for a position with your organization.

I look forward to hearing from you.

Yours sincerely

Daniel Stewart

Enc.

Exercise 9

Designing a CV

Make your CV as simple and clear as possible. Try using different font styles and sizes or use a basic border. Try the layout given or use one of your own. The important part is to make sure that it contains all the relevant information.

CURRICULUM VITAE

Daniel Stewart

Date of Birth: 17 May 1979

19 Garland Street
CHICHESTER
West Sussex
PO21 9JJ

Telephone: (01243) 786655

EDUCATION AND QUALIFICATIONS

Senior School Henry Thornton Comprehensive, Chichester, West Sussex

GCSE Examinations passed – June 1998

Subject	*Grade*
Sports Studies	A
English Language	C
English Literature	C
Mathematics	C
History	D
Geography	D
Combined Science (double award)	D/D

Further Education Chichester Sixth Form College

BTEC GNVQ Advanced Level in Leisure and Tourism – Results expected in July/August 1999

This course replaces the old BTEC National Diploma in Leisure and Tourism and spans a very broad range of subjects relevant to leisure and tourism. A number of assignments are required and these form part of the final result. In addition to these assignments there are a number of external examinations which must be passed. I have successfully completed all of the assignments for all subjects and am currently awaiting the final results of examinations sat this term.

This qualification is judged to be equivalent to A-level standard and it is possible to gain entry to university with suitable grades.

WORK EXPERIENCE

An important part of this course is to gain practical experience and a number of work placements were arranged for this purpose:

The Bee's Knees Leisure Centre, Chichester
I worked here for two weeks in the fitness suite, helping to monitor the safety of clients. I was also responsible for making bookings and answering the telephone.

The Tourist Information Centre, Guildford
I worked in the centre for two weeks and helped with the day-to-day running of the organization, ensuring that sufficient information was available, helping to answer customer queries, answering the telephone and making telephone enquiries on behalf of members of the public.

EMPLOYMENT HISTORY

For the past two years I have worked on a part-time basis at a local leisure and sports centre. My responsibilities include booking in clients, dealing with cash and credit card transactions, maintenance of the fitness suite and checking on the condition and safety of all sports equipment.

HOBBIES AND INTERESTS

I enjoy a wide range of sports including football, swimming, badminton and squash. During my spare time I like to travel as much as possible, I read a good deal and enjoy the cinema and theatre.

ADDITIONAL INFORMATION

I have a current First Aid certificate, gained within the last 6 months.

I have a provisional driving licence and am due to take my driving test in September 1999.

REFEREES

Mrs Roz Slaughter, Chichester Sixth Form College
Mr John Mason, The Tourist Information Centre, Guildford
Mr Andrew Swinburne, The Bee's Knees Leisure Centre, Chichester

Exercise 10

Memorandum layout

We have seen how business letters are formatted. When sending messages in the form of memos *internally*, it is not necessary to include the name of the company. The language in which memos are written is not as formal as with business letters.

- Try the following layout. Record the layout as a macro. It is *very* simple to do. I will give you instructions on how to record a macro in Word for Windows; if you are using a different package, simply look in the help menu.

1. Select a New File.
2. Click on *Tools* then select *Macro*.
3. Click on *Record* and give your macro a name.

A box with symbols, rather like a tape recorder, will appear on the screen. If this is in your way, simply use the mouse to drag it to a new position.

You are now ready to record your Macro. Type the following:

MEMORANDUM

TO:

FROM:

DATE:

SUBJECT:

- Click on *Stop*.
- Click on Tools and select Macros – click on the name of the macro you have recorded. Now click on Run and the memo will be reproduced.
- Now type a suitable memorandum.

MEMORANDUM

TO: Tony – Health and Safety

FROM: Dennis Taylor, Chief Training Officer

DATE: 11 November 1998

SUBJECT: Accident in Sports Hall 2 – 10/11/98

Dear Tony

You should be aware that a serious accident occurred yesterday at 2.30pm. It involved Mr Jason Kennedy and he sustained a broken ankle. Mr Kennedy is claiming that he slipped on something that had spilled onto the floor of the sports hall.

The hall will remain closed until you have investigated the matter. I want you to check the whole surface and if anything was spilled I want to know exactly what it was.

I will wait for your full report before contacting our insurance company. I have questioned the cleaners who insist that the floor was cleaned with a non-slip product.

The last thing we need at the moment is bad publicity and we must ensure that our members' safety is paramount.

Please get back to me **ASAP**.

Dennis

Exercise 11

Designing a data capture form suitable for a leisure centre

This should be a membership form. Think of *all* the details you may require in order to keep a full record of members' details. Write down everything you can think of that might be useful.

When you are sure that you have covered everything, use a word processing or desktop publishing package. Give your leisure centre a name and try to find a suitable picture. This can either be Clip Art or you can use a scanner if you have one available to you.

Try varying the style. Once you have completed and saved one form, try changing it, being a bit more adventurous. Keep the original intact so that you can choose the better one. The example given on page 58 uses tables, with only one row but many columns. Shading has also been used to improve the overall effect.

Exercise 12

Mail merge

A mail merge allows you to key in one standard document, such as a letter, and merge it with a data file, holding names and addresses, to produce personalized letters. This has the very obvious benefit of saving time and, providing the letter is correct, will ensure that all letters are accurate and of a standard format.

The two documents (files) required for a mail merge are called *main* (primary) and *data* (secondary) files.

The following instructions assume that you are using Microsoft Word. If you are using a different type of software you will still have the capability to produce mail merged letters; simply look at your help menu.

Mail merge involves three steps:

1. Creating or modifying a main document (usually a letter)
2. Creating or modifying a data source
3. Creating a merged document.

LEISURE DOME

North Pier
BRIGHTON
East Sussex
BN15 8JJ
Telephone: 01375 87878

MEMBERSHIP APPLICATION FORM

NEW MEMBERSHIP/RENEWAL		DATE	/ /
MEMBERSHIP TYPE	SINGLE	GROUP	FAMILY	UNDER 16	OAP
TITLE		INITIALS		SURNAME	
ROAD					
TOWN					
COUNTY					
POSTCODE		TELEPHONE			
DATE OF BIRTH	/ /	AMOUNT PAID	£		
METHOD OF PAYMENT	CREDIT CARD	CASH	CHEQUE	STANDING ORDER	

MEDICAL DETAILS

(Please complete as appropriate)

GP NAME:
ADDRESS:
TELEPHONE:
HEALTH: POOR/FAIR/GOOD/EXCELLENT
MEDICATION:

Please indicate which of the Centre's facilities you are likely to require:

Tennis Courts/Badminton Courts/Squash Courts/Gymnasium/Fitness Suite/
Swimming Pool/Sauna/Toning Tables/Restaurant/Bar/Sportswear Shop

Signed: ______________________________

To create or modify the main document, click on *Tools*, *Mail Merge*, and then click on *Create a Main Document*. Then click on *Form Letters*. If you are in a new document you may choose this option. Then click on *Close*. Key in your letter. Save this on completion.

Each set of related information in a data file makes up one record. For example, a record in a customer mailing list contains all the information relating to that customer. The different types of information, customer name, postal address, etc., are called 'Fields'. Each field in the data file has a unique name. The field names are seen at the top of the field columns in the data table and are known as 'header records'.

HEADER RECORD	NAME	ROAD	TOWN	COUNTY	POSTCODE
DATA RECORDS	Mr Smith	1 Green Street	Swindon	Wiltshire	WS81 7KL
	Mrs Jones	2 North Street	Chichester	West Sussex	PO19 8JJ
	Ms Jeffries	17 The Fairway	Midhurst	West Sussex	GU19 7JG
	Dr Spock	15 Steinway	Chichester	West Sussex	PO19 7JK

To create the data source, click on *Tools*, *Mail Merge*. Then click on *Get Data* under *Data Source*. Click on *Create Data Source*. The usual fields used appear in the window on the right. Choose the ones you do not wish to include by highlighting them, and delete them by clicking on *Remove Field Names*. You may also add fields that you wish to include by keying in the new data names and clicking on *Add Field Name*.

- When you have completed this task save the data file by pressing *OK* and giving it a data name.
- You will then get a message to say you have no data records. Click on *Edit Data*. The data form will appear on the screen and you will be able to fill in your data records under the appropriate headings using the *Tab* key to move between fields. At the end of the record click the *Add New* button and repeat. When you have entered all records click on *OK*.
- The main document will now return to the screen. Position your cursor where you want your first insertion. Click on *Insert Merged Field* and highlight the field you require. Press *Enter*. Continue to do this until you have all the fields you require in your main document. *Save*.

- Go back to *Tools*, *Mail Merge*, and click on *Merge the Data with the Document*. Now print the merged document.

In order to get the benefit of mail merge you will need a reasonably sized data file. Mail merge is one of the most commonly used processes and if you can master it you will be in great demand!

Exercise 13

Using tabulation

By default, a tab stop is placed at every ½" across the page. Each time you press the tab key [⇆] the cursor will move ½". This is very useful for indenting paragraphs or writing reports. For other work, specialized tabs must be made.

- Try the following exercise. Before typing in text, set the following tab stops: Left tab at 2". Middle tab at 3.75". Right tab at 5.25".
- All of the tab stops set are aligned left; if you prefer, you can change the alignment.
- The example in Figure 4.4 uses Microsoft Word for Windows.
- The Tab instructions can be found by clicking with the mouse on *Format* from the main toolbar at the top of the screen.
- So, you first select *Format* and then *Tabs*. The computer will then display the tabs options.
- Click on *Clear All* to remove all default tab settings. You can now select the tab positions and add the alignment. In the example we are using, leader dots or dashes are not appropriate so you should select *1 None*. Each time you enter a new tab stop you should click on *Set*. See Figure 4.4 for the end result.
- Now simply type in the position where you wish the indent (tab) to stop, and select the alignment you want. For this example you should use the *left* alignment option. Click on the *Set* option.
- Set all remaining tabs in the same way. When you are satisfied that all the correct stops are listed, you can click on *OK*.

- You are now ready to begin the exercise. Type in the text as shown:

HOLIDAY PRICES

HOTEL NEW DOLMEN – MALTA

(ALL PRICES BASED ON TWIN BEDDED ROOM)

(BED AND BREAKFAST)

DEPARTURE	NIGHTS	
DATES	7	14
14 May–28 May	405	539
29 May–7 June	365	515
8 June–28 June	379	539
29 June–6 July	385	545
7 July–17 July	425	699
18 July–18 August	419	615
19 August–11 Sep	389	575

- Save and print your work.
- Adjust the left hand tab stop to 1.5" to allow more room; the result should allow for you to amend as follows:

DEPARTURE DATES	NIGHTS 7	14
14 May–28 May	405	539
29 May–7 June	365	515
8 June–28 June	379	539
29 June–6 July	385	545
7 July–17 July	425	699
18 July–18 August	419	615
19 August–11 September	389	575

The more you use tabs, the easier they will become.

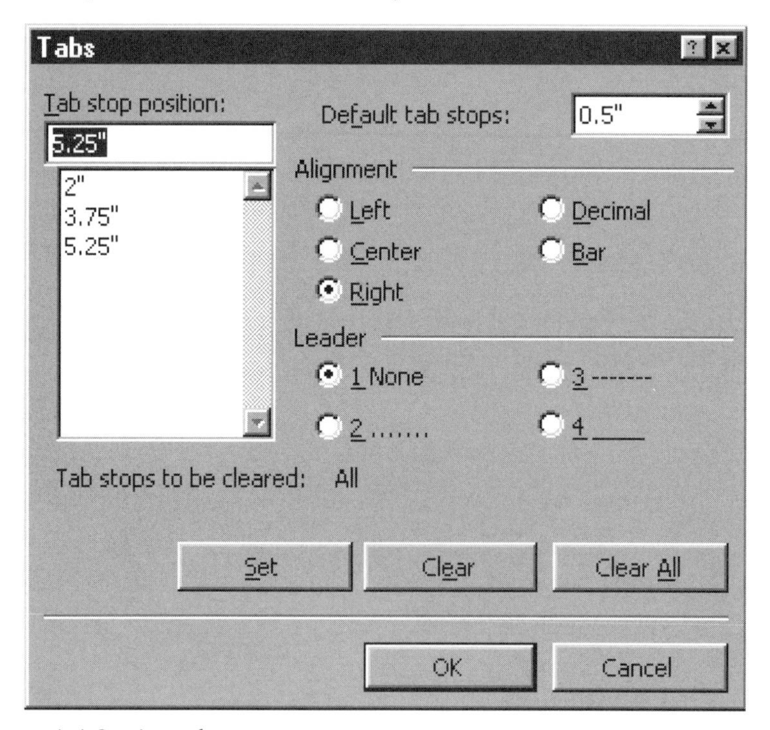

Figure 4.4 Setting tab stops

Exercise 14

Using borders

- Experiment with different types of borders. The Borders options will be found under Format from the main toolbar at the top of the screen.
- You will need to define where you wish your border to be.
- First, highlight the whole table, including the main heading. You can do this by using the mouse. Position the mouse where you wish the border to start. Hold down the left button and 'drag' until the whole area is highlighted.
- Now select *Format* and *Borders* and the options shown in Figure 4.6 will appear.

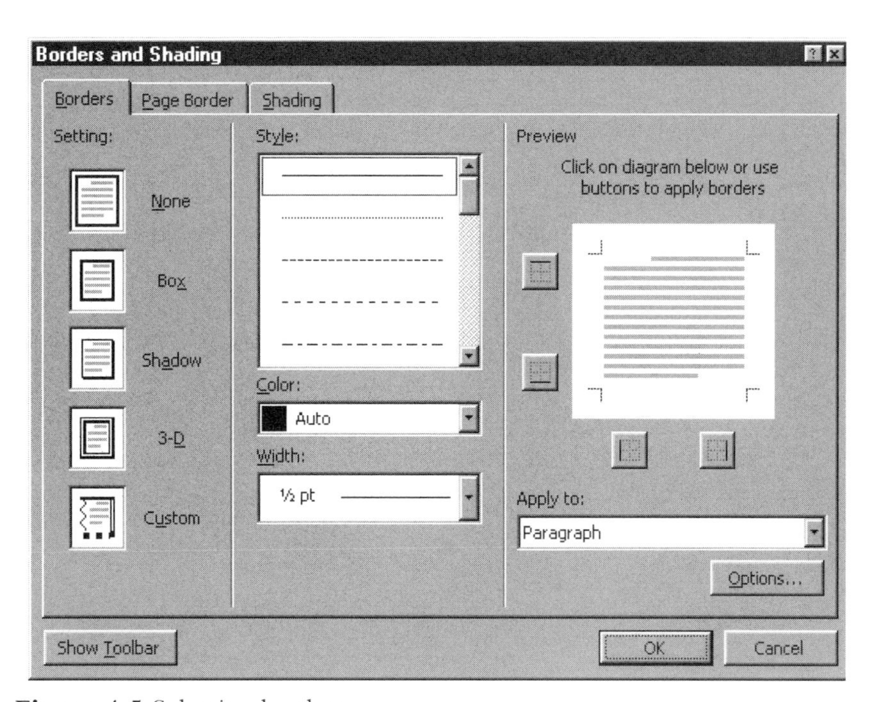

Figure 4.5 Selecting borders

- You can select the type of border and width of the line(s). You can vary the colour if you wish. Simply make your selection and watch the results. If you are not happy, repeat the process and make a fresh choice.

Place a plain border around your work as follows:

HOTEL NEW DOLMEN – MALTA

(ALL PRICES BASED ON TWIN BEDDED ROOM)

(BED AND BREAKFAST)

DEPARTURE	NIGHTS	
DATES	7	14
14 May–28 May	405	539
29 May–7 June	365	515
8 June–28 June	379	539
29 June–6 July	385	545
7 July–17 July	425	699
18 July–18 August	419	615
19 August–11 September	389	575

Spreadsheets

Spreadsheet software is wonderful! It can make even the least mathematical of us produce figures that add up and make sense. In addition, we can produce charts and/or graphs to highlight our findings. The software holds the key to everything you will ever need to calculate; all you need to do is find out how to get the most out of the software.

As with word processing application software, there are many spreadsheet packages available and the way in which you use them will differ from package to package.

Don't be afraid to try! All you have to do is enter the figures onto a spreadsheet and save your work before you practise. By doing this you have lost nothing even if things go horribly wrong. You will find that you learn more by trial and error. Computers aren't fragile and you won't break them by pressing the wrong key.

Exercises will be provided which will test your skills. Solutions will be given so that you can see whether you are on the right track.

If you can use a spreadsheet package which is compatible with your word processing package, you can always insert part or all of the spreadsheet and graphs into a word processed report, giving it a very professional appearance.

The next few pages contain seven exercises that will help you practise your skills.

Exercise 1

Totalling columns and rows

- Create a spreadsheet using the titles and data given. You may need to adjust the column width. The method of achieving this will vary depending on the software you are using. If you have a mouse, you should try positioning the cursor on the line you want to move. Hold down the left button and *drag* it in the desired direction – left to decrease and right to increase.

STUDENT:
NAME:
DATE:
TITLE:

VALUE OF GOODS SOLD OVER A 4 WEEK PERIOD

	MON	TUE	WED	THU	FRI	SAT	WEEKLY TOTAL
WEEK 1	£140.85	£350.00	£140.99	£265.97	£235.00	£350.88	
WEEK 2	£287.09	£235.77	£256.88	£368.22	£365.72	£365.11	
WEEK 3	£198.81	£344.25	£234.98	£245.99	£300.45	£344.91	
WEEK 4	£143.88	£198.88	£178.76	£200.07	£179.76	£275.43	
DAILY TOTALS							

1. Save your work to file, keeping the document on screen.
2. Find the weekly total of goods sold. If you are using a mouse, position the cursor in the cell holding the figures for week one on Monday (£140.85). Hold down the left button and carefully drag the mouse to the right so that all figures for week one are highlighted *including* the column for the weekly total. Click on the Σ icon. The result of the calculation should now be displayed. You can practise this by using the same method for finding the totals for the remaining weeks, and also the daily totals and the overall total for the 4 weeks.
3. Save your work using a different file name, leaving the original intact.
4. Print your spreadsheet.

- Check your answers. Are they in the correct format, i.e. pounds sterling? If not, highlight the range and select the currency option.
- Are the results correct? If not try to see if you can find out why.
- Are you satisfied with the overall layout of your work? If not, you can go over it and embolden and/or underline your work. You might like to change the type or size of font.

STUDENT:
NAME:
DATE:

VALUE OF GOODS SOLD OVER A 4 WEEK PERIOD

	MON	TUE	WED	THU	FRI	SAT	WEEKLY TOTAL
WEEK 1	£140.85	£350.00	£140.99	£265.97	£235.00	£350.88	£1483.69
WEEK 2	£287.09	£235.77	£256.88	£368.22	£365.72	£365.11	£1878.79
WEEK 3	£198.81	£344.25	£234.98	£245.99	£300.45	£344.91	£1669.39
WEEK 4	£143.88	£198.88	£178.76	£200.07	£179.76	£275.43	£1176.78
DAILY TOTALS	£770.63	£1128.90	£811.61	£1080.25	£1080.93	£1336.33	**£6208.65**

Try changing the contents of the cells holding the data for value of goods sold and you will see that the totals will automatically be revised.

Try drawing some conclusions from the results of your data. Have any patterns emerged? Monday seems to be a poor day for trading. Totals for Week 4 are particularly poor. If you were running a small business and there was such a large reduction, you would want to find out why.

Exercise 2

Addition, subtraction, multiplication and division

- This easy exercise deals with two-cell arithmetic. Write your name and today's date in row 1.
- Type the headings in columns A, B, C and D, and enter the data. You will need to adjust the width of the columns to allow sufficient room for the headings.
- Save your work giving it a suitable file name and retain the spreadsheet on the screen ready to give the computer the formulae it needs.

ADDITION	SUBTRACTION	MULTIPLICATION	DIVISION
8766	762	876	1234
1212	768	45	543

1. Position the cursor in the first answer cell – leaving a clear row.
2. Give the correct formula, i.e. **8766 + 1212**. How you go about this will depend on the software you are using. For example, if you are using Microsoft Excel you would leave the cursor in the answer cell and type a plus symbol **+** . Then move the cursor into the first cell which holds **8766**. Now enter the operator; in this case we are using the addition operator, so press the + key. Now move the cursor to the second cell for calculation, i.e. the one holding 1212, and press enter. The answer will now be displayed.
3. Use the same method for the remaining calculations. You will have to alter the operator: – for subtract, * for multiply by and / for divided by.

ADDITION	SUBTRACTION	MULTIPLICATION	DIVISION
8766	762	876	1234
1212	768	45	543
9978	–6	39420	2.272559853

You will notice that the answer for the division calculation takes the answer to many decimal places for greater accuracy. Although there will be times when such a degree of accuracy is required, it is often possible to limit the number of decimal places. You should adjust the format so that an appropriate number of decimal places is displayed.

Exercise 3

Using percentages

- Type your name and today's date in row 1.
- Type in the headings as shown and enter the figure for the original price in row 3 column A.

ORIGINAL PRICE	DISCOUNTED PRICES – ORIGINAL PRICE			
	LESS %	LESS %	LESS %	LESS %
£1536.00	10	12.5	15	20

- Find the amount by which the price has been discounted:

1. Position the cursor in the answer cell and (if using a mouse) type the plus symbol +.
2. Move the cursor into the cell holding the original figure (£1536.00) and type the subtraction symbol –.
3. Move the cursor back into the cell holding the original figure, press the function key F4 (this makes the cell *absolute* – a cell is only made absolute if it holds a 'constant', i.e. a figure that does not change) and type the multiplication symbol *.
4. Move the cursor into the cell holding the first discount (10) and type the division symbol /.
5. Type 100 and press enter.
6. The first answer should now be displayed.
7. If this has worked correctly then you can copy this formula for the remaining discounts. How you do this will vary, depending on the software you are using. With Microsoft Excel you simply move the cursor to the first answer cell then move it to the corner of the cell until a plus sign (+) appears. Drag the mouse using the left button until the whole range is highlighted. This takes practice. Once you have the results for each of the discounts you may save and print your work.

ORIGINAL PRICE	DISCOUNTED PRICES – ORIGINAL PRICE			
	LESS %	LESS %	LESS %	LESS %
	10	12.5	15	20
£1536.00	£1382.40	£1344.00	£1305.60	£1228.80

Exercise 4

Further percentages

In Exercise 3 we knew what the percentage was. In this exercise, we know what the percentage represents in cash but do not know the percentage that this represents. Therefore the formula we use must be modified.

- Type in the exercise as shown:

Prices have increased for the past 5 years.

Find the percentage increase for each year, based on the original figure for 1994.

	1994	1995	1996	1997	1998
	£15,000.00	£15,300.00	£17,544.00	£18,500.00	£19,975.00
Increase					
Percentage increase					

- Find the amount of increase, i.e. by how much the price has risen since 1994:
  1. Position the cursor in the answer cell and type +.
  2. Move the cursor into the cell holding £15,300.00 (for 1995) and type the operator –.
  3. Now move the cursor into the cell holding £15,000.00 (for 1994) and press the F4 key to make the cell absolute.
  4. Once you have this answer, copy the formula across to get the increased for 1996, 1997 and 1998.

- Calculate the percentage increase:
  1. Position the cursor in the answer cell and type +.
  2. Move the cursor into the cell holding £15,300.00 (for 1995) and type the division operator /.
  3. Now move the cursor into the cell holding £15,000.00 (for 1994).
  4. Type the multiplication operator * and type in 100.
  5. Press enter and the result should read 2%.
  6. Use this method for each of the remaining increases.

Prices have increased for the past 5 years.

Find the percentage increase for each year, based on the original figure for 1994.

1994	1995	1996	1997	1998
£15,000.00	£15,300.00	£17,544.00	£18,500.00	£19,975.00
Increase	£300.00	£2544.00	£3500.00	£4975.00
Percentage increase	2.00	16.96	23.33	33.17

Exercise 5

Finding the break-even point (no profit/no loss)

■ Enter the data exactly as shown and adjust the column width as necessary.

TOTAL FIXED OVERHEADS PER YEAR	£15,000.00
PRODUCTION COSTS PER UNIT	£2.45
SELLING PRICE PER UNIT	£4.50

UNITS	REVENUE	OVERHEADS	PROFIT
100			
500			
1000			
1500			
2000			
2500			
3000			
3500			
4000			
4500			
5000			
5500			
6000			
6500			
7000			
7500			
8000			

■ Calculate the column for revenue:

1. Position the cursor in the first answer cell, i.e. for 100 units, and type the + symbol.

2. Now move the cursor into the first units cell, i.e. 100, and type the * operator.
3. Now move the cursor into the cell holding the selling price per unit and press the F4 key.
4. Press enter and the answer will be displayed.
5. Copy this formula for the remainder of the column, i.e. up to and including 8000 units.

■ Calculate the column for overheads:

The fixed annual overhead will remain the same, whether 1 or 1,000,000 units are produced.

The other overhead is variable, i.e. the cost of manufacturing one unit multiplied by the quantity produced.

1. Position the cursor in the cell where you wish the first answer to appear and type the + symbol.
2. Move the cursor into the cell holding the fixed overhead figure of £15,000 and press the F4 key to make the cell absolute.
3. Now press the + operator.
4. Move the cursor into the cell holding the number of units (100) and press the * operator key.
5. Move the cursor into the cell holding the manufacturing price per unit and press the F4 key.
6. Press enter and the answer will be displayed.
7. Copy this formula for the remainder of the column, i.e. up to and including 8000 units.

■ Calculate the profit:

1. Move the cursor to the first answer cell for profit (100) and type the + symbol.
2. Move the cursor into the first cell holding the revenue for 100 units and type the – operator.
3. Move the cursor into the first cell holding the overheads for 100 units and press enter.
4. The profit for 100 units will now be displayed.
5. Copy the formula for the remainder of the column.

TOTAL FIXED OVERHEADS PER YEAR	£15,000.00
PRODUCTION COSTS PER UNIT	£2.45
SELLING PRICE PER UNIT	£4.50

UNITS	REVENUE	OVERHEADS	PROFIT
100	£450.00	£15,245.00	–£14,795.00
500	£2250.00	£16,225.00	–£13,975.00
1000	£4500.00	£17,450.00	–£12,950.00
1500	£6750.00	£18,675.00	–£11,925.00
2000	£9000.00	£19,900.00	–£10,900.00
2500	£11,250.00	£21,125.00	–£9875.00
3000	£13,500.00	£22,350.00	–£8850.00
3500	£15,750.00	£23,575.00	–£7825.00
4000	£18,000.00	£24,800.00	–£6800.00
4500	£20,250.00	£26,025.00	–£5775.00
5000	£22,500.00	£27,250.00	–£4750.00
5500	£24,750.00	£28,475.00	–£3725.00
6000	£27,000.00	£29,700.00	–£2700.00
6500	£29,250.00	£30,925.00	–£1675.00
7000	£31,500.00	£32,150.00	–£650.00
7500	£33,750.00	£33,375.00	£375.00
8000	£36,000.00	£34,600.00	£1400.00

Estimating

- Estimate how many units need to be manufactured in order to break even, i.e. no loss but no profit. You may either write down your 'guess' or create another row on the spreadsheet and type it in.
- Once you have done this save the file and print a copy of the spreadsheet.
- After you have estimated the quantity required in order to break even, try using the computer's 'goal seek' tool. How you go about this will depend on the software you are using. The method for Microsoft Excel is as follows:
- Click on *Tools* and select *Goal Seek* and the following selection box will appear:

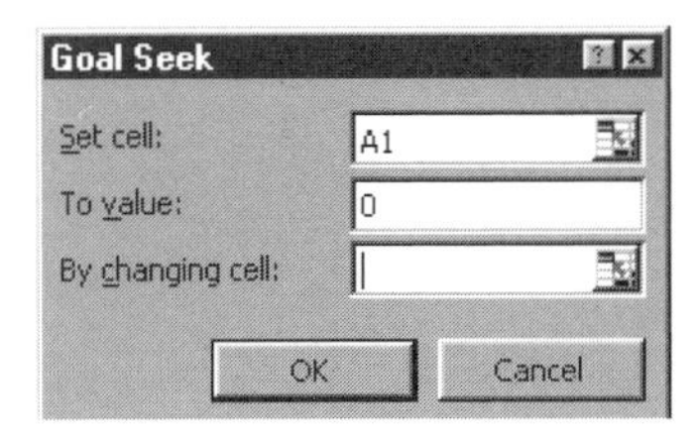

- Click on Set cell. Now click on the cell holding the profit for 7500 units.
- You now need to move the cursor into the area to select the value. Type 0 (this is because we are looking for break-even point).
- Now move the cursor into the area by changing cell and either click on the cell holding 7500 units, or type in the cell address, i.e. column/row.
- Click on OK.
- You will need to reformat this cell for an integer value, i.e. a whole number with no decimal places (we cannot manufacture a fraction of one unit).

Model answer:

TOTAL FIXED OVERHEADS PER YEAR	£15,000.00
PRODUCTION COSTS PER UNIT	£2.45
SELLING PRICE PER UNIT	£4.50

UNITS	REVENUE	OVERHEADS	PROFIT
100	£450.00	£15,245.00	–£14,795.00
500	£2250.00	£16,225.00	–£13,975.00
1000	£4500.00	£17,450.00	–£12,950.00
1500	£6750.00	£18,675.00	–£11,925.00
2000	£9000.00	£19,900.00	–£10,900.00
2500	£11,250.00	£21,125.00	–£9875.00
3000	£13,500.00	£22,350.00	–£8850.00
3500	£15,750.00	£23,575.00	–£7825.00
4000	£18,000.00	£24,800.00	–£6800.00
4500	£20,250.00	£26,025.00	–£5775.00
5000	£22,500.00	£27,250.00	–£4750.00
5500	£24,750.00	£28,475.00	–£3725.00
6000	£27,000.00	£29,700.00	–£2700.00
6500	£29,250.00	£30,925.00	–£1675.00
7000	£31,500.00	£32,150.00	–£650.00
7317	£32,926.50	£32,926.65	£0.00 – Break-even
8000	£36,000.00	£34,600.00	£1400.00

Exercise 6

Using charts

- A group of boys have a bag containing 50 sweets to share. The older boys decide they should have more than the younger children, so they are shared out like this:

Name	Sweets
Tom	12
James	10
Garry	7
Philip	7
Michael	6
Ashley	5
Tiny Tim	2
Even Tinier Tim	1
	50

What kind of chart would be most suited?

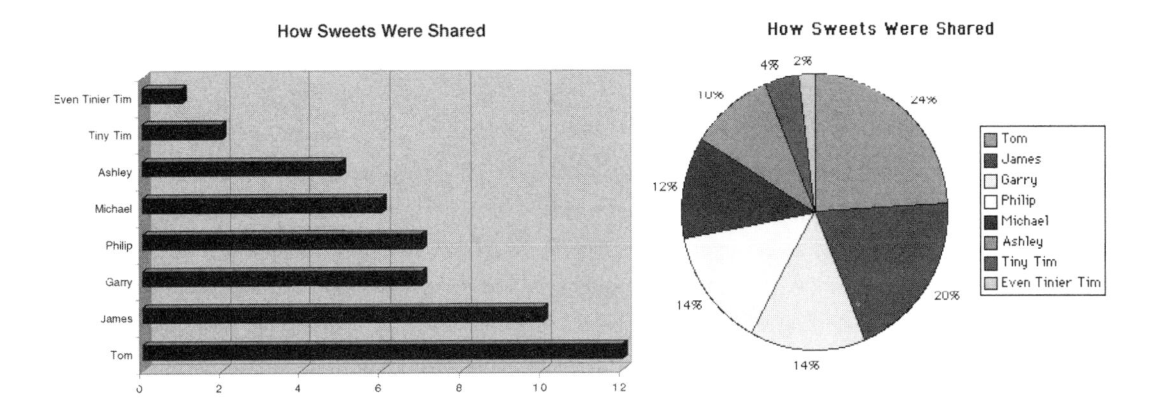

Figure 4.6 Bar chart

Figure 4.7 Pie chart

Either of these two charts would be suitable to show the data. You will notice that the pie chart gives the results in percentages, while the bar chart shows the actual number of sweets each boy had.

Exercise 7

Averages

We covered the subject of averages under the Application of Numbers examples. If you need to refresh your memory, refer back to pages 25–6.

- Enter the following data into a spreadsheet and give the correct commands in order that the computer can calculate the mean average score. Then calculate by how much each student's score deviates from the 'norm'.

TEST RESULTS FOR MATHEMATICS EXAMINATION – MAXIMUM POSSIBLE 100

STUDENT	RESULT	DEVIATION FROM AVERAGE
CAROL HOLMES	95	
DANIEL NEWMAN	82	
TOM FIELDING	80	
SIMON BAILEY	76	
TRACEY JONES	68	
MARK OLDHAM	62	
MICHAEL HARRIS	59	
CLAIRE PAYNE	50	
CAROLINE BORGATTI	50	
JOHN GREENWOOD	45	
TREVOR MACDONALD	40	
JAMES MACDONALD	35	
CLARE GREENE	30	
PETER MARCH	22	
TOTAL		
MEAN AVERAGE SCORE		

1. Find the total of all scores. Highlight all scores *including* the blank cell for *total* and press the Σ symbol.
2. Find the mean average score for students. Position the cursor in the answer cell for the mean average and press =. Move the cursor to the cell holding the total of scores and use the / operator. Now type in the frequency, i.e. there are 14 students so type *14*. Now press enter and the result will be displayed. Format the cell holding the mean average, to display just two decimal places.
3. Find by how much each score deviates from the mean average figure. Position the cursor in the answer cell and type +. Now move the cursor into the cell holding the result for student 1 (Carol Holmes) and use the – operator. Now move the cursor into the cell holding the result of the mean average and press the F4 key to make the cell

absolute. Now press the enter key and the deviation from mean average score will be displayed for the first student. Replicate this formula by copying it for the remainder of the students. Format the whole column for deviation to just two decimal places.

4. Check your results – if you total the column for deviation from the mean average it should be 0.00.

TEST RESULTS FOR MATHEMATICS EXAMINATION – MAXIMUM POSSIBLE 100

STUDENT	RESULT	DEVIATION FROM AVERAGE
CAROL HOLMES	95	38.29
DANIEL NEWMAN	82	25.29
TOM FIELDING	80	23.29
SIMON BAILEY	76	19.29
TRACEY JONES	68	11.29
MARK OLDHAM	62	5.29
MICHAEL HARRIS	59	2.29
CLAIRE PAYNE	50	–6.71
CAROLINE BORGATTI	50	–6.71
JOHN GREENWOOD	45	–11.71
TREVOR MACDONALD	40	–16.71
JAMES MACDONALD	35	–21.71
CLARE GREENE	30	–26.71
PETER MARCH	22	–34.71
TOTAL SCORE	794	0.00
MEAN AVERAGE	**56.714286**	
MEAN DEVIATION		0.00

Note: The above calculations were done using a computerized spreadsheet. The deviation from the mean average was limited to just two decimal places. The total deviation from the mean average was then calculated and this gave a figure of 0.00. The mean deviation from the 'norm', i.e. mean average result, was calculated by dividing the total deviation by 14. If you use a calculator to solve this problem you will gain a different answer: total deviation is 0.06 and the mean deviation is calculated by dividing 0.06 by 14. The result on the calculator will be 0.0042857. Slight discrepancies in results are fairly common.

Databases

What is a database?

Computerized databases are designed to store records in respect of people, organizations, stock, etc. An integrated database will be made up of a number of different files and used by individuals and/or departments.

The alternative to a computerized system would be a manual system where records are stored either in filing cabinets or possibly in a card index system. Such systems have many drawbacks:

- Any unauthorized person can access records if the cabinets or rooms are not locked.
- If authorized personnel access records, it is possible that they will remove a record from the file and it can be lost forever.
- The record may be replaced in the wrong order.
- It is only possible to file records by a single category, e.g. alphabetical order or chronological order.

Providing a computerized system has been properly set up and security checks are in place, none of the above could happen. The biggest benefit of computerized systems is speed of access. Another big plus is that records can be stored in many ways, i.e. not just in alphabetical order. We will look at this in more detail when we begin to design our database system.

Using a database is one of the most common requirements of businesses within the leisure and tourism industry. If the organization is large, then the likelihood is that you will not be required to design and set up the database but merely learn how to access records.

If you work for a smaller organization then it would be very useful if you could have sufficient knowledge to actually design and set up a database system which would meet the information needs for the whole organization.

We cannot talk about computerized database systems without first being aware of the Data Protection Act.

Any organization that maintains a computerized database must first check with the Data Protection Registrar to see whether they need to register and also to find out how people and/or organizations contained within the system must be protected.

The Data Protection Act was introduced in 1984 to protect the interests of the subjects on whom data were being kept in computer files. This Act is constantly being updated, so you should always obtain a copy of the latest rules to ensure that you do not break the law.

The basic principles with which data uses must comply are as follows:

1. Data must be obtained and processed fairly and lawfully.
2. Data must be held only for lawful purposes which are described in the register entry.
3. Data can be used or disclosed only for those or compatible purposes.
4. Data must be adequate, relevant and not excessive in relation to the purpose for which they are held.
5. Data must be accurate and, where necessary, kept up to date.
6. Data must be held no longer than is necessary for the purpose for which they are held.
7. Data must be kept secure.

Individuals have the right to see and challenge data being held about them. A small fee is often required and a maximum limit will be set by the Data Protection Registrar.

If the data can be proved to be inaccurate, legislation exists to ensure that corrections are made. However, there is no automatic right to any compensation, even if you can prove that incorrect, possibly harmful data are being kept.

The Data Protection Registrar will deal with organizations not maintaining records within the rules set down.

We have now discussed the requirements of keeping data, but where do they come from?

Data are (no, I haven't made a mistake – the word 'data' is plural, even though it doesn't sound it!) collected from many different sources. The person who comes to read your gas or electricity meter will 'capture' a reading, either by writing the data onto a special form or using a hand-held computerized capture system.

If you go along to join a leisure centre, you will be required to complete a membership form. The data 'captured' will be used to form your record within a membership file. Without a form, or at least suitable headings under which data are displayed, the meaning of a data item can be quite misleading.

To take an example, the word 'White' could refer to anything:

- somebody's surname
- the colour of hair, skin or teeth
- a species of shark.

Once data have been gathered, they must be processed and only then will they have any use. Processed data is called 'information'. Once data have been processed they can be displayed as either part of or the whole of a record, with suitable headings.

Try to collect some samples of data capture forms – these can be found just about everywhere. The layout will help you to design your own form. The design is important as it should be very clear what data are required.

Look at the Membership Application Form for the Leisure Dome on page 58. This is a fairly typical layout and it will help the leisure centre to capture the necessary details to form a whole record. These are:

- membership number and whether it is a new membership or a renewal
- type of membership
- date of registration
- name of applicant (broken down into title, initials and surname)
- address of applicant (broken down into road, town, county and postcode)
- telephone number (you could include a daytime as well as a home number)
- date of birth
- amount paid for registration
- method of payment
- medical details
- details of applicant's GP (broken down into name, address and telephone number)
- medical health
- any medication taken by the applicant.

Another useful field would be special sporting or relaxation interests.

There may be more data which would be of interest – can you think of any?

Once you have decided on the data required, you can then create a database file to store your data.

The structure of a computerized database is as shown in Figure 4.8.

Figure 4.8 Structure of a computerized database

A *database* can be made up of one or many *files*. These files may be linked together if required. We will look at how to do this later in this chapter.

Each *file* will contain a number of *records* which will relate to an individual, organization, stock records, etc.

Each record will be broken down into *fields*. The benefit of breaking down each record is that the record can be stored under any number of field headings. When the database user wants to find a record they are not then limited to finding it by checking only on one field, e.g. surname. We will look at a number of benefits this brings within this chapter.

The field will be made up of *characters*. For example, a surname would be a simple character string, a date of birth would be in the format DD/MM/YYYY, money would obviously be in the correct format, i.e. numeric with two decimal places, age would also be numeric but with no decimal places, i.e. an integer.

You are now ready to create your first database file.

The method you use will obviously depend on the software package you are using, but all database software should have more or less the same capabilities. If you are unsure, see if there is a demonstration available or look at the help menu.

- Decide on the requirements of your database file.
- Decide how many fields you are going to need for your record purposes.
- Decide on the type of characters that will go to make up each field and also the maximum length of field. For example, if one of your fields is for a surname, you will possibly require a maximum of 20–25 characters in case of double-barrelled names.
- Select a new file and give it a suitable name.
- Break down the record into field names, giving the type of character and maximum width of field. Continue to do this until you have noted every field name.
- Save the file and you are now ready to begin keying in the data.

For this first exercise we will keep it simple.

Exercise 1

Creating a database file

Field Name	Character Type	Maximum Width
Membership_No	Numeric (integer)	6
Membership	Character	1 ('O' for Old or 'N' for New)
Type	Character	1 ('S' for Single, 'G' for Group, 'F' for Family, 'U' for Under 16 and 'O' for OAP)
Title	Character	4
Initials	Character	3
Surname	Character	20
Date_of_Birth	Date	Computer will do this automatically
Road	Character	30
Town	Character	20
County	Character	20
Postcode	Character	8
Telephone_Day	Character	12
Telephone_Home	Character	12
Sum_Paid	Numeric (with 2 decimal places)	6
Date_Paid	Date	Computer will do this automatically
Method	Character	2 ('CC' for Credit Card, 'CA' for Cash, 'CH' for Cheque, 'SO' for Standing Order)
GP_Name	Character	20
Address	Character	50
Telephone	Character	12
Health	Character	1 ('P' for Poor, 'F' for Fair, 'G' for Good or 'E' for Excellent)

You must now store these details by saving the database file.

Data should be entered in the sequence given. When you have finished entering data belonging to the first record, ensure you have a fresh sheet before beginning on the second and subsequent records.

Records to be entered:

123456 N S MR G K HAMILTON 06/05/1980
17 WILLINGDON DRIVE EASTBOURNE EAST SUSSEX
BN23 9MM 01323 814072 01323 128765 300.00 12/10/1997 CC
DR J HORNE EASTBOURNE HEALTH CENTRE WILLINGDON ROAD EASTBOURNE BN23 8MN 01323 811212 G

121212 O S MS J F HORNETT 12/11/1968
28 METCALFE AVENUE NEWHAVEN SUSSEX GN17 8JJ
01273 355988 01273 559877 300.00 17/04/1998 SO
DR JACKSON NORTH SHORE ROAD BRIGHTON BN26 7HH
01273 876987 E

014353 O F MRS H SMITH 01/03/1968
17 NORTH STREET BURGESS HILL SUSSEX BN87 7JJ
01444 987776 01444 98776 240.00 10/09/1998 CH
DR K PINKERTON HIGH STREET BURGESS HILL BN87 7JK
01444 876567 F

000987 O S MISS T L MORTIMER 08/07/1975
13 GOODWOOD CLOSE MIDHURST WEST SUSSEX GU29 8JH
01243 812218 01730 814987 300.00 12/09/1998 CA
DR HUDSON MIDHURST HEALTH CENTRE MIDHURST
GU29 7JH 01730 812121 E

123457 N O MR K M RODENT 25/12/1935
1 THE FAIRWAY MIDHURST WEST SUSSEX GU29 9JH
01243 814545 01730 817654 200.00 10/12/1997 CA
DR HUDSON MIDHURST HEALTH CENTRE MIDHURST
GU29 7JH 01730 812121 P

123458 N O MRS K RODENT 01/01/1939
1 THE FAIRWAY MIDHURST WEST SUSSEX GU29 9JH
01730 817654 01730 817654 200.00 10/12/1997 CH
MR HUDSON MIDHURST HEALTH CENTRE MIDHURST GU29 7JH 01730 812121 F

093245 O U MR P POTHURST 17/12/1987
FLAT 7 23 HIGH STREET CHICHESTER WEST SUSSEX PO19 8JJ
01243 837467 01243 817876 100.00 17/12/1997 CH
DR K PATEL CHICHESTER HEALTH CENTRE CHICHESTER
PO19 7JK 01243 876543 E

- Add more records. Enter your own details and those of friends and family.

1. Now save the file and print a single copy which shows all the fields and data.
2. Sort records in ascending order on the field of Membership_No and print.
3. Search the file for people who live in *East Sussex*, i.e. County = East Sussex, and print the results.
4. Search for all members who paid for the membership *before* 12/12/1997 ready for renewal notices.
5. Search for any members whose health is poor, i.e. Health = P, and print record(s) so that they show the following fields: title, initials, surname, date of birth, GP name and address.

Try producing records and display the data under suitable headings. You might like to adjust the size of the font.

You will now have practised designing and creating database files. You have sorted, searched and printed. The next stage we will tackle is deciding how files can be integrated.

Exercise 2

Linking files

To save you too much typing we will deal with files with just a few records.

This exercise uses three files and relates to stock held in a leisure centre.

The first file we will create is designed to store details of items held in stock. The second file will hold details of suppliers. The third file will hold details of orders placed with suppliers.

Once we have created these files we will need to link them together for purposes of ordering and paying bills. In order that files can be linked, each file must contain at least one field on which it can be linked.

File name	*Stock_file*	
Field name	*Character type*	*Maximum width*
Stock_Ref	Character	5
Supplier_Ref	Character	5
Quantity	Numeric (integer)	5
Unit_Price	Numeric (2 decimal places)	6
Description	Character	30
Size_Colour	Character	15

File name	*Supplier_file*	
Field name	*Character type*	*Maximum width*
Supplier_Ref	Character	5
Contact	Character	20
Name	Character	30
Road	Character	40
Town	Character	30
County	Character	30
Postcode	Character	8
Telephone	Character	12
Payment_Terms	Numeric (integer)	1 (1 for cash with order 2 for 7 days of receipt 3 for 14 days of receipt 4 for 28 days of receipt)

File name	*Order_file*	
Field name	*Character type*	*Maximum width*
Order_No	Character	4
Qty_Ordered	Integer	6
Supplier_Ref	Character	5
Stock_Ref	Character	5
Order_Date	Date	Will be done automatically by computer
Goods_Due	Date	Will be done automatically by computer

By using three files instead of one very large one, it is possible to link them together when required, e.g. in the case of ordering goods. If you are simply doing quick stock-taking, however, you would not need to know all the additional data and so the stock file alone would be of far more use.

In order that files may be joined together, the field names on which they will join must be identical as to the type of characters and width of field.

We will create just three records in each of the files. This will be sufficient to see how the link will work.

- Create a new file and call it STOCK. Set up your database file to hold the following records:

00345 D3465 12 SWEAT SHIRTS 23.99 LARGE BLUE LOGO

11863 D4377 3 BADMINTON RACQUET 79.87 WHITE FLASH

11876 D4377 4 TENNIS RACQUETS 100.50 CARBON FIBRE

- Save the file.
- Create a new file and call it SUPPLIER. Set it up to hold the following records:

D4377 JAMES TAYLOR DUNLOP WHOLESALE HORSHAM TRADING ESTATE HORSHAM WEST SUSSEX BN34 8MN 01403 876598 3

D3456 JOHN MACMILLAN PRINT SUPPLIES HOLMBUSH TRADING ESTATE MIDHURST WEST SUSSEX GU29 8JG 01730 8145767 4

D1978 RANJIT VERGHESE SPORTS R US NORTH STREET CHICHESTER WEST SUSSEX PO20 8JK 01243 557764 2

- Save the file.
- Create a new file and call it ORDER. Set it up to hold the following records:

04564	20	D3465	00345	19/10/1998	18/12/1998
04565	10	D4377	11863	20/10/1998	10/12/1998
04566	5	D4377	11876	28/10/1998	18/12/1998

- Save the file.

Look up the instructions for your particular software and do the following:

- Join the table in the Stock file to the table in the Supplier file and to the table in the Order file on the common field of *Supplier_Ref*.
- If you view the result, you should have the full details from each file.
- If this does not work, you should look at the individual files and check that the data are correct. You may have used the wrong field name or mis-typed the data in one or more of the files.
- Once you have successfully joined the files, print the full results.
- Now try producing a report.
- Designing and using databases do take some practice but it is well worthwhile; there is an ever-growing demand for people who can design databases, especially within small organizations.

Presentations

We have now looked at using word processing, spreadsheet and database software and by now you should be experts! The next type of software we need to explore is something that will aid presentations. Of course, not everybody will have this software at their disposal, so I will give you some helpful hints for impressing an audience.

During the course of assignments, there comes a time when everybody's heart sinks! You have to stand in front of the whole class and give a presentation and you just know that somebody is going to give you a hard time.

Be prepared

Think of the audience. If you are really not looking forward to taking part, try to draw as much attention away from yourself as possible. If you don't have software which will allow you to give a really slick slide presentation, complete with sound bites, then prepare handouts and acetates for use on an overhead projector to illustrate and summarize your talk. This focuses the audience's attention on the points you are making rather than on you as a person.

Don't read every word from a page! If you feel embarrassed, it is tempting to put your head down and read from a sheet. This will lose you marks, and if you should lose your place you will feel even more of an idiot! Write notes as a memory jogger. Use very large print for these notes so that you can read them easily by just glancing down from time to time.

Remember – although you feel as though you are the only one who is quaking in their boots, there will be lots of other students out there, trying to put on a brave face.

The material you produce for your presentation should look very professional. Don't be tempted to use very technical words. You must be absolutely certain that you understand all the points you are trying to get across. There is nothing more embarrassing than being questioned on one or more points you have raised and having to confess that you don't actually understand them!

Using slide presentation software

The method used will vary depending on the software you are using. If we take an example of using Microsoft Powerpoint, you will have the possibility of selecting a blank presentation from a range of slide layouts. Some of these are designed to hold text only and some a combination of text and pictures. You should never overcrowd a slide. Use bullets to highlight each item you are dealing with and you can then talk in greater detail.

If you choose a mixture of graphics and text you can either select from the various Clip Art graphics which are held or alternatively scan in a picture of your own.

You simply create one slide after another. You can change the order in which they will appear. The next choice you can make is whether to use the mouse manually to select when you want the next slide in the sequence to appear or to set a time limit so that the next slide will come up automatically.

You can apply colours and patterns to your slides and vary the way that the slides are introduced, e.g. a chequerboard effect going up, down, coming from the left or the right. The choices are excellent.

If you become really expert at using this type of system you may like to include some sound. This can be done by using sound from CDs, sound clips held by the computer or a microphone so that you can do your own commentary. Experiment as much as you can: the more practice you get, the slicker and more professional your presentation will be.

5

Sample Assignments

Gaining Application of Number and Information Technology Core Skills

As we have already discussed, it should be possible to achieve most if not all of the core skills by working on the mandatory and optional units of the GNVQ Intermediate or Advanced Level in Leisure and Tourism.

We will take one unit for Advanced Leisure and Tourism: *Business Systems in the Leisure and Tourism Industries (Advanced)*.

This unit is in three parts:

1. Investigate and evaluate administration systems in leisure and tourism organizations.
2. Investigate and evaluate communications systems in leisure and tourism organizations.
3. Investigate and evaluate information processing systems in leisure and tourism industries.

This particular unit has been chosen since it is one which lends itself to information technology, and manual systems can be identified and compared with computerized systems.

When you are given the three assignments for this unit, you will either be told to find your own organization to investigate or possibly be given a full case study on which to base your investigations and findings.

Under Element 5.1 you are required to perform and/or show a good understanding of the following Performance Criteria:

1. Explain what the main purposes of quality standards are in leisure and tourism organizations.
2. Identify and give examples of administration systems supporting the function of leisure and tourism organizations.
3. Evaluate the effectiveness of an administration system in supporting one function in a selected leisure and tourism organization and summarize findings.
4. Suggest possible improvements to the operation of the evaluated system.

Evidence indicators for this assignment are quoted as follows:

1. A brief report on administration systems in leisure and tourism organizations. The report should outline in general terms the main purposes of quality standards, and should identify administration systems supporting the functions of leisure and tourism organizations. The report should be illustrated with four examples of administration systems supporting routine functions, and one example of a system supporting a non-routine function.
2. A summary of findings based on an evaluation of the effectiveness of an administration system supporting one function in a selected leisure or tourism organization. The findings should cover all the categories listed in the range 'Evaluate the effectiveness'.
3. Suggestions for possible improvements to the operation of the evaluated system.

Remember, when writing a report, the layout must be correct:

1. Introduction

1.1 XXXXXXXXX

  1.1.1 XXXXXXXXXXXX

1.2 XXXXXXXXXXXX

1.3 XXXXXXXXXXXX

2. XXXXXXXXXXXXXXXXXX

Reports should never be written in the first person, i.e. *not* 'I decided to…' but 'it was decided…'.

Produce a front cover with a suitable graphic and remember to include your name, the assignment title, the lecturer's name and the date the work is submitted for marking.

Include a page index and remember to add an appendix and bibliography in which you will note any magazines, textbooks, etc. that you have used. A sample report follows.

1. Introduction

A brief report has been requested on the subject of administration systems within leisure and tourism organizations.

An investigation has been carried out on a wide range of administrative systems in both the leisure and tourism industries. Results of findings will be detailed in four separate sections which will cover the following:

1.1 The main purpose of quality standards within leisure and tourism organizations.
1.2 Examples of administrative systems within the industry will be identified and explained.
1.3 An evaluation of the effectiveness of a number of administrative systems will be given. This evaluation will deal with one function in a selected leisure environment and one within a selected tourism organization.
1.4 A summary will also be included that will contain suggestions for possible improvements to the existing systems as evaluated.

2. Quality standards

Quality standards exist within all sections of the leisure and tourism industry. It is the responsibility of all management to ensure that staff receive training and are fully aware of each of the standards that must be maintained.

2.1 *Health and safety*

Quality standards are constantly being updated, and so the organization must be sure that it conforms to the latest British and international standards. Very strict rules apply to the storage and preparation of food and teams of inspectors have the right to carry out inspections without prior notice. Any organization found to be breaking hygiene rules will be warned and will often be made to close the premises until they can prove that work has been done in order to conform to all the rules.

2.1.1 Refrigerators and freezers must be maintained at the correct temperatures and cooked and uncooked food must not be stored together. Hand washing and drying facilities must be freely available and hair should be tied back.
2.1.2 Samples of food may be kept for testing.
2.1.3 Proper ventilation is essential and heating should be at a comfortable temperature.
2.1.4 All surfaces should be free from grease and floors should have non-slip surfaces.
2.1.5 All sporting facilities must have a good safety policy and trainers should be on hand to assist with any equipment and/or exercises.
2.1.6 A first aid kit should be available and checks should be made to ensure that the contents conform to the rules.

2.2 *Investors in People*

This particular standard is not essential but is much prized by employers. In order to gain this award the employers must prove that their staff training policy is excellent.

3. Examples of administrative systems

The purpose of administrative systems within any organization is to have in place methods and facilities which will deal with the day-to-day running of the organization.

3.1 *Administrative systems supporting routine functions*

3.1.1 Finance

No organization can function without the control of finance. If we take the example of a tour operator, the administration covering finance is quite complex.

We need only look at some of the different parties involved in transactions to appreciate this fact:

Customer Travel agent Tour operator
Insurance Currency conversion Airline staff
Airline caterers Hoteliers Transfer transport

Keeping track of all the incoming and outgoing monies is vital. Apart from a legal requirement to keep financial records for purposes such as tax, etc., without complete records the organization would not be able to keep track of how much *they* are owed and how much they need to pay. Another obvious drawback would be that cash flow analysis would be impossible, meaning they could make no plans based on future projections.

There are numerous methods which can be used for controlling and recording financial transactions. In these days of computerization, the vast majority of organizations transfer funds electronically. Providing security checks are firmly in place, this means that there is less scope for accidental or intentional misappropriation of funds.

Spreadsheet and accountancy computer software is available to cope with the day-to-day requirements of any organization.

3.1.2 Human resources

Human resources, often referred to as Personnel, are another administrative system common to any organization. Human resources deal with interviewing and employing new staff, disciplining existing staff, training staff, staff welfare and monitoring staff development generally.

Staff records are often held in the human resources department and these will be used, in conjunction with the wages department (finance), to pay staff salaries.

3.1.3 Customer services

The administrative systems that work within the customer services section of leisure and tourism organizations deal primarily directly with customers. A company policy of standards should be in place and all employees should be made aware of this.

Even in the best-run organization things can go wrong, and the customer services department will deal with any customer complaints. Common complaints which occur in the tourism industry often relate to delays in take-off times. Airlines normally have a policy of allowing for delayed travellers to receive a set sum of money for food etc., based on the length of the delay.

When holiday-makers are unhappy with the standard of accommodation, their first action must be to complain to the holiday representative. The customer will often take up their case with the travel agent and/or tour operator on their return.

All complaints must be fully documented.

3.1.4 Quality assurance

Quality assurance administration is designed to ensure that customers have no cause for complaint in the first place. The quality assurance may be part of a British or internationally set standard, or simply standards and/or guidelines set by the organization.

If we take an example of a leisure centre, the types of standard which must be maintained are:

- Health and safety
- Helpful, well qualified staff
- Well maintained equipment
- Clean floor and wall surfaces
- Good value for money
- Efficient booking systems
- No delays, i.e. clients must not be kept waiting
- An accident book in case of any minor or major accidents.

These standards for quality assurance must be written down as part of company policy, and all staff should be fully aware of them.

When any problems arise and anything falls below the required standard, occurrences must be fully documented and every attempt must be made to overcome the problem and promote customer satisfaction.

3.2 *Administrative systems supporting non-routine functions*

As well as dealing with day-to-day problems, administrative systems must also be in place in order to deal with the 'out of the ordinary'.

3.2.1 Emergencies

Guidelines and policies must also be in place for any emergency which may occur. In a leisure centre the following should be in place and *all* staff will be aware of procedures:

- Fire drills should be regularly carried out so that staff know what to do in order to evacuate the centre safely of all clients and staff.
- A map of the leisure centre should be displayed in each room in order that clients can identify exits from the building.
- Fire exit doors must be correctly maintained and clients should be able to identify these doors clearly as a safe exit.
- Fire alarms and fire extinguishers should be maintained regularly to ensure they are in working order.
- Ideally another source of light will be available in the event of power failure, so that clients and staff can be safely evacuated from the building.
- In the case of swimming pools, the safety measures should be very stringent. Qualified lifeguards should be in place to help any swimmers in difficulty. The temperature of the water should be checked and properly maintained. The levels of chlorine in the water must also be thoroughly checked. Too much added chlorine could lead to breathing difficulties; in this event the pool must be evacuated and closed off.

Once again, any emergency must be well documented. This is a requirement of the Health and Safety Authorities.

The examples given refer only to a leisure centre; emergency procedures for any other type of organization must also be in place.

The travel industry in particular will have very stringent regulations which must be administered.

3.2.2 Accidents

Procedures on how to deal with matters when accidents occur must be in place, and all staff should be aware of such procedures. Qualified first-aiders should be appointed so that there is always somebody available to assess accidents.

There is a legal requirement for an accident book to be kept, and an entry should be made for even minor accidents. The more details that can be documented the better. One reason for this is that the client may want to pursue a claim against the organization. In addition, an exact record of the events which occurred may assist the medical practitioner in the speedy recovery of the patient.

4. Evaluate the effectiveness of an administration system in supporting one function of a selected leisure and tourism organization and summarize the findings

The subject for this section of the report has been based on a small independent leisure centre. The function investigated was the maintenance of membership records.

4.1 *Fitness for purpose*

The management of the leisure centre used to keep details of membership records on a manual card index system. These records have recently been computerized.

There are two computers, connected together via a lap link cable. This allows data to be transferred/shared between the two computers. The software installed on these computers is 'off the peg' Microsoft Office. The operating system is Microsoft Windows '95.

The management employed somebody to advise them on setting up a database system that would help them to keep track of membership. The design for this database was based on their original card index system which contained the following data: membership number, type of membership, title, initials, surname, gender, date of birth, address (road, town, county and postcode), two telephone numbers (daytime and home) and the renewal date for membership.

The organization stated that on the whole they were happy with the new system, although staff training was difficult. Some of the existing staff were concerned for their jobs. They worried that they would not be able to cope with the new system and also that once the data had been entered into the new system their jobs could be at risk.

It was stated that there had been no job losses but that job descriptions of staff had been broadened to allow for greater flexibility.

4.2 *Value for money*

The system chosen would certainly seem to be cost effective. The organization already had the two computers: one in the front office and one in the back. They also had the operating system and Microsoft Office software. Until creating their database system, the only part of this software which had been utilized was the word processing software.

The correct licences are held for software and so the only additional cost was the employment of a consultant to help them design their database system. This system was very simple in design and so the sum involved was quite modest. A lap link cable was also purchased as well as lap link software to allow the computers to communicate. The total cost of these additions was between £400 and £500.

The organization stated that they expected to have off-set this amount very quickly. In the past, client memberships had been allowed to lapse, as, without going through the whole card index system, there was no way of finding which members needed reminding about renewing their membership. The new system allows for very speedy access of records, and the names and addresses in the database are used in order to send mail shots to members whose membership is about to lapse.

The management team were all aware of the Data Protection Act and stated that all records were correctly maintained and the system was secure.

4.3 *Accuracy*

As with any system, the accuracy of data is only as good as the staff who maintain the system. Management stated that the change to a computerized system had given them the opportunity to check the data before it was entered into the new system; they felt that the level of accuracy was very high.

It was stated that records were maintained by computer-literate staff and that searches based on renewal dates were stored in a separate file before being used for mail merge purposes.

4.4 *Efficiency*

It was stated that the efficiency of administration dealing with membership had been greatly improved. The speed with which records could be retrieved was much greater, and since nobody could 'walk off' with computerized records, as they had done with cards from the index system, the system was far more secure. The improved efficiency of renewing membership was excellent.

4.5 *Security*

The organization stated that they were satisfied that their system was secure, since only computer-literate staff used it. However, they stated that they did not use any passwords and that their database was stored only on the computer's hard disk. They did not back-up their system onto another medium.

4.6 *Ease of use*

The organization's opinion was that the system was easy to use. On investigation, however, it was found that a more user-friendly interface could have been used as a data input screen. No validation had been used in order to check registration numbers, e.g. a range check could have been placed on numbers. This would have reduced errors. If the maximum number of members was unlikely to exceed 700, then the range check would concern only records between 1 and 700.

Regular back-ups should be an essential part of the system, and it was surprising that their database advisor had not stressed this point.

4.7 *User opinion*

The users of the system were quite happy. They stated that after some initial problems they felt that the administration was running smoothly and that they had noticed a huge improvement when searching for records.

5. Improvements to the operation of the evaluated system

There are many ways in which the system studied could be improved.

5.1 *Procedures*

The procedures within the computerized system can be improved in many ways. If the administrative system for membership were to be integrated with the booking system, it would be possible to have an efficient accounting system.

To improve the membership system, it is felt that the design of the database could be improved by increasing the number of fields under which records are stored. In case of accident and/or emergency it would be useful to have details of each member's GP. Any special medical problems could also be listed, together with any medication used by the member. A telephone contact number for the next of kin could also be useful.

In addition to increasing the number of fields which go to make up records, the database software could be utilized more fully by applying validation checks as data are entered.

Backing-up procedures should definitely be in place. Data files could be copied onto floppy disks or spooled onto magnetic tape. These disks or tapes should be stored away from the computer and preferably in a fireproof safe. Once any organization's records are computerized, they become their most precious possession. It is always possible to buy new computers and software, but it will not be as easy to regain details of their members and/or clients.

It is strongly recommended that system security is looked at more carefully. Only authorized staff should be able to gain access to computers. Passwords could be set up and issued to staff. These passwords should be changed regularly as further security.

5.2 *Improvements to level of staff skills/expertise*

Although the relevant staff are capable of using the new computerized system, their level of expertise could be improved. With the facilities available, they could make far more use of the computers by learning more of the purpose and capability of the database system. Since it is they who actually use the system, they are best placed to identify any weaknesses or drawbacks. It was discovered that the staff were not given an opportunity to voice an opinion on the computerized procedures.

More time should have been taken at the planning stage to make the membership procedures more efficient and effective.

Now that staff have become familiar with the software, they should be encouraged to undergo further training in order to get the most out of the system and improve the design of the database system.

Guidance notes for students

By word processing your assignment and making it clear that you have a good understanding of information technology, you can provide evidence for many of the IT Core Skills. Information gathered during your investigation of the system should be retained and could be included in an appendix at the end of your report.

Keep original notes and copies of the report *before* final editing. This will prove that you have gained all the IT Core Skills for Preparing Information and many of the Performance Criteria for Processing Information.

Once you have created your own database for a leisure centre, you can provide further evidence through reorganizing information by sorting, etc.

You should also find that you have achieved most of the Performance Criteria of the element which evaluates the use of information technology.

From this you can see that virtually all of the information technology Performance Criteria have been achieved during the course of one small assignment.

The next assignment in the Business Systems Unit is to

investigate and evaluate communications systems in leisure and tourism organizations.

I do not intend to write the assignment for you in report format but offer the following guidance.

The best way to approach the requirements of the Performance Criteria which go to make up this element is first to research the subject and keep any notes or subject material for inclusion in the appendix as you did with the first assignment.

You should begin with an introduction, explaining what you intend to do within the report, and then go on to break the report down into separate, numbered paragraphs.

The first criterion is to explain the functions and purposes of communications systems within the leisure and tourism industry.

The *function* of communications systems is to support the management and operation of organizations to allow for communications both internally, i.e. to other departments and personnel within the organization, and externally, i.e. to outside organizations and individuals.

The *purpose* of communications systems is to ensure that information is always communicated to the right organization or person, whether within the organization or externally. It is always a good idea to use diagrams to show how such communications might work.

The next Performance Criterion requires you to describe and give examples of types of communications systems used by leisure and tourism organizations.

The types of communications system used in order to pass messages and/or information will obviously vary, depending on the proposed recipient(s).

The types of system can be broken down into one-way and two-way communications.

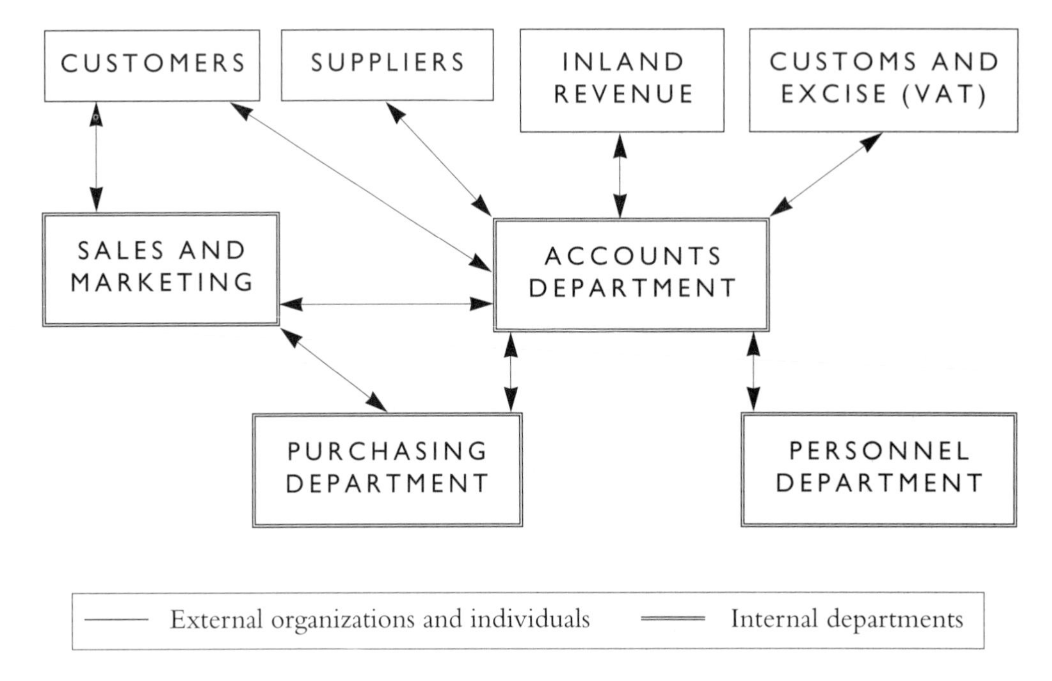

Figure 5.1 Communications system

One-way communications systems include:

- Signs – these may be used to good effect only where the person is able to read the sign. You can never guarantee that everybody will read the sign. For example, signs in offices, leisure centres, etc., are often ignored.
- Display panels – this type of panel is commonly used at airports and railway stations and gives the traveller details of the time and point of departure. Most travellers are able to make use of such information; for visually impaired people, it is less useful.
- Written correspondence – letters, memoranda, reports, etc., fall into this category. These are an effective way of communicating information.
- Public address systems – the quality of public address systems varies a great deal. They rely on the system having good-quality speakers, and the person delivering the message must have a clear voice.
- Computer-generated speech – this means of communication is gradually becoming more common. Again, the quality varies a great deal, depending on the system being used.

Obviously, with all one-way systems of communication there is (with the exception of written communication) no way of directing questions back to the sender of the message.

Two-way communication systems include:

- Face-to-face communication – i.e. speaking, either on a one-to-one basis or a one-to-many basis. This obviously has the benefit of allowing all parties to pass information and queries back and forth until everybody is satisfied that the message has been clearly understood.
- Telephone – we are all familiar with using the telephone and this is an effective way to send and receive messages. In addition to the normal telephone system with which we are all familiar, i.e. one-to-one, telephone conferencing is now becoming popular. This allows for several people to link up, allowing them all to take part in the conversation.
- Intercom systems – these are useful for relaying information within a confined area. For example, intercoms are used in offices and factories to relay messages. This has the drawback of not being private, i.e. it is 'broadcast', so that everybody within earshot is able to hear the message.
- Mobile radio – mobile radios are used when either one or both parties are not close to any other means of communication. For example, country rangers often use mobile radios.
- Video conferencing – this is a very sophisticated means of communication. In order for video conferencing to take place, each party must have the necessary equipment set up, including a computer system, with communications software, a camera and a microphone. This system has the benefit of allowing many people to take part in the meeting without the need to leave their offices, saving time and money.
- Inter-active computer programs – there are many types of inter-active computer programs. Some may be a way of gathering data, e.g. the computer will ask the user for an answer to a question and the user will type their response. Other systems include communication systems that allow the user to use e-mail. The user may receive and send messages to a 'mail box', where messages can be picked up when required and printed.
- Sign language – when we think of sign language we normally think of it as a means of communication with the deaf. Sign language is useful where the noise level is too high for individuals to communicate and there are no other means available. For example, on-course bookmakers use a type of

sign language known as 'tick-tack'. Sign languages using a series of flags (semaphore) can be used at sea or on land.

The next requirement is to explain how the development of electronic technology has affected communications systems in leisure and tourism.

Technology is changing and improving all the time, and computers now have an enormous influence within the leisure and tourism industries. The travel industry in particular would suffer greatly if computer systems were to fail.

Such systems include:

- Computer reservation systems – we are all familiar with these. We walk into a travel agent or ticket booking centre and the operator will use the computer system to find out availability. They will tell us the location, price, etc., giving us the opportunity either to accept or reject the reservation. If we accept the reservation the booking can be made instantly by means of the computer.
- Computer networks – it is often necessary for computers to be linked together in order to get the most out of the system. Sometimes they will be linked within a single organization. This is known as a Local Area Network. This type of system will require a file server, designed to store software and data which can be shared by those on the network. It is possible to operate such systems without the use of a modem by using lap link cables, but the system will operate more efficiently if a modem is used.

  Where it is necessary to communicate over a longer distance, a wide area network will be required. This allows people at remote sites to use their computers, with appropriate communications software, to download files if required, or simply send and receive messages.
- Electronic mail systems – these allow users to send and receive messages by using their computers. This system supports both typed messages and audio messages (voice).
- Enhanced telephone systems – the telephone network can be used to communicate by *fax machines*. Each line of text and/or graphic is converted into a series of dots. It is then sent down the telephone line and is converted back into its original format by the receiving fax machine. Modems are required in order to convert the digital signals used by computers into analogue signals (sound waves) as used by most telephone networks. The message will then travel down the telephone line to its destination. Once it arrives, another modem will be required in order to convert the analogue

signal back into digital format so that it can be received and understood by the receiving computer. The *Internet* is another common means of communication via the telephone network. In order to use the Internet, the user must have the appropriate software and will have paid a monthly fee to the line service provider. The Internet allows for messages to be sent anywhere in the world, providing the remote site is also licensed to use the Internet, and the cost will be charged at the rate of a local telephone call. In addition to sending messages, the user can browse the net by entering a subject(s). A search will be made and a great deal of information usually results from such searches.

- Voice comprehension – it has taken some time to overcome problems with voice comprehension by the computer. The early systems required a great deal of training. Each time a word, phrase or sentence was spoken, the words would be keyed into the computer using a keyboard. In this way the system would build up a bank of simple messages. The system has since been vastly improved and it should soon be possible for everybody to use their voice in order to input data and pass messages. Some systems are now available which accept voice input and convert it into type. This is obviously very useful for slow typists and bad news for people who use the word processor for a living!
- Voice generation – some computer systems are capable of generating a 'voice'. There is still a little way to go before this is perfected so that it has a really human quality, but improvements are being made all the time.
- Touch screens – these systems are often used in exhibition halls and allow the user to select from a menu the type of information they require. Touch screen technology is also useful for disabled people who cannot use keyboards. Specialist software has been developed for this purpose.

All of this new technology has improved administration and communication within the leisure and tourism industries. The speed at which records can be accessed has been improved, saving time and money. Fax and electronic mail have largely done away with the need for sending letters, etc., by mail, once again speeding up transactions.

Through computerization, organizations are able to offer a superior, more efficient service to their customers.

The next two Performance Criteria are to evaluate the effectiveness of communications systems used in selected leisure and tourism organizations and summarize the findings; and to suggest possible improvements to the system evaluated.

Evaluate the effectiveness of communications systems used in selected leisure and tourism organizations and summarize the findings.

In order to achieve this you will have to provide proof that you have investigated a particular communications system. This will be partly done by including original notes on the subject, taken at the time of your investigation. These can be included in the appendix of your report.

You have now learned many techniques in presenting your findings to their best advantage. Remember to state clearly and concisely the task you have undertaken. Explain the type of organization you studied and give a little background information before explaining how the communication system works and giving your evaluation of the system.

Suggest possible improvements to the system evaluated.

This is quite a simple task. If you can think of improvements to the organization's present system you should state *what* you suggest and *why* you think it would be an improvement.

Hopefully, by going through two Elements of the Business Systems in the Leisure and Tourism module, you will have gain an insight into how your assignments can be improved and how you can achieve many of the Core Skills Performance Criteria.

You should be able to supply evidence of the Application of Number Core Skills by carefully reading through the requirements and applying them to other assignments, especially for the unit *Finance in the Leisure and Tourism Industries.*

For example, if you study an organization such as a leisure centre and your findings include the financial controls, you can state how they go about controlling their finances and give worked examples. For example, you could show how they would need to find their break-even point.

You might also demonstrate an ability to work out averages, mean, mode and median, and find by how much each data item deviates from the 'norm'.

It is worth putting in a little more effort when doing this as it will save you time in having to complete additional assignments for the Application of Number Core Skills.

Planning is the key to good assignment work. Discuss with your tutor how you intend to approach the subject and he/she should be able to give you guidance.

Hopefully this book has given you some useful hints on achieving your GNVQ and the author would like to wish you good luck with your course work and examinations!

Index